unshakeable

unshakeable

the steadfast heart of obedience

jan coleman

BROADMAN
&HOLMAN
PUBLISHERS

Nashville, Tennessee

0-8054-3162-4

Published by Broadman & Holman Publishers,
Nashville, Tennessee

Published in association with the literary agency of Janet
Kobobel Grant, Books & Such, 4788 Carissa Ave.,
Santa Rosa, California 95405.

Dewey Decimal Classification: 248.84
Subject Heading: CHRISTIAN LIFE \ OBEDIENCE \
GOD—WILL

Unless otherwise noted, all Scripture quotations have been
taken from the Holman Christian Standard Bible, © 2000
by Holman Bible Publishers. Other versions cited are NIV,
the Holy Bible, New International Version, © 1973, 1978,
1984 by International Bible Society; TLB, The Living Bible,
copyright © Tyndale House Publishers, Wheaton, Ill.,
1971, used by permission; The Message, the New Testament
in Contemporary English, © 1993 by Eugene H. Peterson,
published by NavPress, Colorado Springs, Colo.; and
KJV, King James Version.

1 2 3 4 5 6 7 8   09 08 07 06 05

dedication

To my husband, Carl, who chooses to live rightly no matter what it costs. Your love for the Lord inspires me more than you know.

acknowledgments

To my adult Sunday school class at Sonrise Church. For your challenging comments as we dug into God's Word every week. And for all the candid confessions and prayer requests that became windows to your truth-seeking souls.

To my editor Len Goss at B&H who helped me brainstorm this project on a napkin over dinner in Nashville and coached me with tips for the book proposal. Thank you for believing in me and my passion to share this message.

And to all of you who came forward to offer your story, eager for the world to know there are blessings when we step over to God's side. Thanks for your honesty.

To Ken Pense, my counselor friend, who shared a cup of coffee with me at La Bou and sent me off with renewed excitement for kingdom living.

table of contents

All my requests are lost in one,

"Father, thy will be done."

–Charles Wesley

introduction

WARNING: If you're bent on running your own life, don't read this book. It could cause side effects for which there is no easy antidote. It's loaded with stories of ordinary people with little in common but a crisis of faith—their self-will in a standoff with God's will. Difficult choices followed, but in time, so did great spiritual reward.

A few stories are my own.

The best source material comes from a writer's own adventures. When my husband, Carl, urged me to tackle this topic, he said, "Jan, I'm amazed at all you've been through, the way you learned to do the right thing and leave the results to God. There's a book in that."

Out popped my creative antenna, sending out feelers that chased through my memory grasping for anecdotes. One latched on in full color right away—me at a crossroad in my Christian life, confused and cheerless, begging my counselor for the directions to Happiness Hotel. She offered a vague smile and this: *Obedience is God's answer to your problem.*

Now there's a proverb for you. The dictionary describes a proverb as a short, pithy saying in frequent and widespread use that expresses a basic truth or practical precept.

Pithy, by the way, means meaty and packed with substance. The essentials or *heart of the matter*.

"If you keep My commands you will remain in My love," said Jesus in John 15:10. It can't get more to the heart of the matter than that.

I thought about the beginning of my rocky obedience journey, convinced that living a righteous life is draining. Much like paddling upstream in a leaky canoe, laboring against a stubborn current watching everyone else going with the flow, picnicking in their designer rafts.

Constant toil with no hint of fun. And for this sanguine gal, fun fuels her emotional food chain.

Questioning filled my early faith life. How much *more* must I do to please God, how much *harder* do I have to try to be good? *And when do I get my reward?* As if it's a heavenly Oscar with my name on it. *Best performance in a difficult role.*

It's so not about performance, but it took me a while to catch on. As someone once said, "Quit trying so hard. That's religion, and it'll do you in every time. I've been there, done that, and have the T-shirt."

Then my path crossed some Christ followers who were really "loving God" and "keeping his commandments." People who figured out that God's plan is not one of perfection, but progress, steady steps toward what we know is right. They made the choice to align themselves with Christ fully, move to his side of every debate, and love him with all their heart, mind, soul, and strength.

And in the *loving* him, doing the right thing begins to come naturally as the heart grows willing. Once we are firmly rooted in our Lord, we begin to comprehend the breadth, width, height, and depth of his love, a love that seeks our highest good, no matter what.

Epiphany time for Jan. *It would be smart for you to hang out with these kinds of people, observe, listen, ask questions, and pick up some Solomon-type wisdom.* So that's what I did.

You'll meet them in the following pages. Some of my old and new friends will inspire you with their stories of standing firm: doing the right thing huts. They're ordinary people like you and me who came to their crossroad, a moment of truth, and discovered: *The purpose of my life belongs to God, not me. All he asks is for me to trust and obey. OK, I can do that because I know he loves me.*

Ordinary people who believe what Moses told the wanderers in his care: "This is what the LORD commanded you to do, that the glory of the LORD may appear to you" (Lev. 9:6).

CAUTION: You may need your sunglasses to read this book. The glory of the Lord gleams from every page.

We can't inherit Christian character, but we can be inspired to change and grow by the testimony of others. It starts with a decision to *risk* loving God and let him transform the heart. The reward for obedience is God revealing himself through our faithfulness.

It's the best choice this former fool ever made. While I once panted after the praises of others—and would do almost anything for applause—there is now only one whose approval matters. There is no greater ambition than that.

Ponder these words of the prophet Jeremiah: "Stand at the crossroads and look; ask for the ancient paths, ask where the good way is and walk in it" (6:16).

How's that for pithy? Simple basic truth with king-size wisdom.

And the reward comes next: "And you will find rest for your souls" (6:17).

Obedience is God's answer to your problem.

the bargain with God

chapter 1

My daughter tilted her head, scrunched her nose, and gave a faint sigh. "I'm so confused." I knew what would come next. "What do you think about all this, Mom?"

With an eye on her one-year-old son picking at his scrambled egg, Amy sat at my kitchen table asking for my opinion—should she give her husband another chance or not.

My lips refused to move as if they were fused with superglue. How could I say what was in my mother's heart? *Don't go back to him. You deserve better than what you've had with him.*

For once, I was glad to be speechless.

She lifted Andrew out of the high chair and turned to me. "You OK, Mom?"

"Just pondering . . ." and inwardly sneering at the thought of her reconciling with Jesse now.

Three months prior to this kitchen conversation, Amy called in desperation, "I can't take it anymore." For months she'd been telling me all about it—the angry exchanges, the ugly words. At first, I offered strategies for her to try, but finally Jesse lost control and hit her.

My maternal hinges came undone.

"That's it! We have to get her out of there," I urged—OK, demanded—of my husband, Carl. In our short fifteen months of marriage, he had not seen me dig in my heels and insist on my way. We were still honeymooning.

At my sudden assertiveness, Carl raised an eyebrow. "Are you sure it's the right thing?" Carl is always tossing that statement at me, and frankly, I had no concern for *rightness* at that moment. To appease him I consulted our pastor. He agreed that if Amy were in a potentially dangerous situation, we should rescue her from it, so off to Southern California we went.

I had 386 miles of desolate freeway to *think*. I tried every diversion—the oldies station on the radio, scanning magazines, shooting off Trivial Pursuit card questions to Carl—but nothing worked. I wrestled with the old enemy propaganda that always hits me when I'm weak: *"If only."* If only my marriage hadn't failed, and her dad had stuck around. If only I'd agreed to let my prodigal daughter back home the last time she begged me for another chance instead of insisting she enter another program. If only I'd done this or that and not the *other* thing.

Before she ran away to Southern California with Jesse.

There's nothing like miles of nothingness to mull over our *should-haves* and *could-haves*. They grind so finely into guilt.

Amy never consulted me about getting married. At the tail end of her rebellious period, she was beginning to let down her defensive walls. God had begun to soften her bruised heart after her father's abandonment. She and Jesse were two troubled kids seeking solutions to their pain and problems in each other's arms.

Both had made decisions for Christ in their youth, and since Jesse's brother just happened to be the pastor of a church in town, they felt convicted about their living arrangement and asked for a quick ceremony following the church service. They told me after the fact.

Another reason to be peeved at Jesse. How could he leave me out of my daughter's wedding day (as if Amy was not a party to it)?

The marriage was a disaster from the start. A foundation built on sinking sand. No surprise to me.

Now Amy was home, with me and Carl, a man who values my daughters more than their long-absent father does. Her head began to clear, and she grew more confident, more settled. She began sifting through her past, examining her foolish choices, and allowing God to mend the broken places.

God loved her and had a purpose for her life; it was enough to cling to for now. Just take it day by day, she echoed to herself.

That morning she thanked me for paying for counseling sessions. "Carol is helping me understand about personal boundaries. I've never had any, never felt worthy enough. I'm beginning to see that God accepts me despite all the yucky things I've done. I have value and he loves me just as I am."

My heart ached for the way her young life had been ravaged, her innocent youth wasted on disastrous choices. From age fifteen she was gone from the house so much her room became the guest quarters.

So many missed years with my daughter, but now she was home with me again. For the first time we began to talk as friends. We could make up for lost time and have so much fun together now.

What do you think, Mom, should I give my marriage another try? "I have no feelings left for him anymore," she admitted, "but he seems so different now. He is listening, hearing what I say to him. Last night he asked for forgiveness for his anger. He's determined to get to the root of it and heal. He wants another chance. And, he is—my husband."

"Yes . . ." unfortunately, I thought.

Amy offered Andrew a grape, and with moistness in her eyes she said, "I know God hates divorce."

In my mother/parrot fashion, I'd reminded both my girls of this time and again—*marriage is for life.*

"What would you do, Mom?"

Ask me anything but that, please. I like thinking your marriage never happened. Sometimes I hate reality.

What *would* I do? When her father had begged me for another chance, I'd given in over and over. *Yes, let's start anew. Of course, I'll forgive the infidelity. You're my husband, my mate. Together we'll find out what's making you do this.*

In the end he dumped me for another woman, had two more children, and faded out of our lives, as if we never existed.

What if she were one of my *friend*s asking me this question and not my daughter? A friend who finally stood her ground and it shook her husband up so that he came to his knees and saw the light. She saw a glimmer of hope that the marriage could be restored.

How would I advise this friend? Especially if she felt the tug on her heart from God to trust him again and saw his genuine concern to preserve the family, to try and become the husband he should be? If he was ready and willing to do it God's way.

Would you stammer for an answer, Jan?

No. I would gladly blurt out with confidence: *Be obedient.* It's been my standard response, my tried-and-true answer, life tested. God blesses our obedience. *God always blesses obedience.*

But I couldn't cough up those words for Amy. They wouldn't squeak out, not with the tae kwon do going on in me, the skirmish between the right answer—the godly answer—and what my mother's heart cried out to say.

Don't do it. He's not sincere. I wish I'd left your father after he hurt me so much, but I stayed in the marriage. I believed him when he apologized and asked for another chance. I gave him my heart, my life, and he left us anyway. Your marriage was a mistake. You deserve better than this. Just walk away. I'll help you begin again.

Just then the phone rang and saved me for the moment. It was Jesse wanting to talk with little Andrew.

• • • •

Have you ever had a brush with God over doing the right thing? Join the club. My experience is not that unique—the questions, the struggles, the testing. We are constantly wrestling with putting God's purposes ahead of our own.

A few months ago Carl charged through the back door after an elder board meeting. "Got a minute? I want to share what happened today." Those who know him best call Carl, *Mr. Reserved*, so when he comes bouncing in, it's my cue to sit down and be quiet. I might learn something.

"Ken Pense came to the meeting today," he told me between gasps. Ken is a Christian counselor in town, and the elders asked him to enlighten them on some issues Christians are facing today.

"People come to me with marriages about to break up, addictions they can't conquer, bitterness issues," Ken reported. "I always start out with the same question: Where are you in your relationship with God? They say they know the Lord, they have the assurance of heaven, but they are burned out trying to make life work. When we get down to the root issues, what is required of them, they don't want to hear it. Our churches are full of people whose faith doesn't translate to their lives."

For weeks my husband chattered about this. "It's not about just changing behavior," he said. "It's about renewing your mind. It's about loving God enough to follow him, to do his will, no matter what."

"Sounds like a new book to me," I quipped, and it got me reminiscing about my obedience journey.

It started when my unexpected—by me—divorce devoured my dreams like a swarm of insects, and I turned to Christ. (You can read the story in my first book *After the Locusts*.) Soon after I found myself in a counselor's office trying to sort through the mess of my life—compounded by the pursuit of an antidote for the pain. A new man.

Mike's attention helped restore my worth as a woman. My heart cried out for love, my body yearned for sexual fulfillment, and my mind for directives to a secure future. "He" seemed the perfect solution.

Except for my recurring state of misery because we'd stepped over the line into sexual sin. No matter how I tried to excuse it—we were in love, etc.—it felt wrong. He suggested marriage to resolve the issue, and I pressed the panic button. The counselor would surely have some strategies for me.

Not so. No advice—or condemnation—only one revolutionary sentence: *Obedience is God's answer to your problem.*

Obedience? For this I'm shelling out seventy-five dollars an hour?

"Go home and ponder it," she suggested, and noted a few Scriptures I might find helpful.

Like Scarlett O'Hara, I was happy to put it off and *think about it tomorrow*. The following night I headed to my 3–D meeting, *Diet, Discipline, and Discipleship*. Ten of us met weekly for weight management and Bible study. In our three weeks I had lost the most weight since I was an emotional wreck with my man problems.

We were in the book of Deuteronomy. The Jews are on the border of Canaan, about to enter the promised land. Moses, who is now 120 years old and would not be coming along, has some farewell words, reminders of the spectacular things God has done for them—the grand rescue at the parting of the Red Sea for one—and that they had committed to obey his laws.

After wandering for forty years, the Israelites were embarking on a new life, leaving one season to enter another. They would need to remember exactly who they were: rebellious and prone to blowing it—big time—but still God's chosen people confirmed by the covenant relationship.

All a puzzle to me, the new believer, and when it came to Scripture, I was still in the Dark Ages. However, once you can reveal your true weight to women, there can be few untouchable issues, so I inquired, "Can someone enlighten me on the covenant relationship?"

Tressa nodded. This gal ran a housecleaning business and spent her days rubber-gloving it through bathrooms with earphones attached for nonstop listening to Christian ministry radio programs. She, even now, is a walking Bible commentary. She tried to explain it in layman's terms, how God chose Israel and considered his people his "treasured possession," not because of their worth but because of what he would do through them.

"Forty years earlier at Mount Sinai, God made a covenant with Israel; they would be a nation through whom the entire world would come to know God. They promised to love and obey the Lord. The covenant is that promise, a sacred pledge, a forever vow."

Oh, like marriage. I looked down at my bare ring finger. Something began to gel in my brain. This was not about my plumpness at all. I was in this study to shed more than bulk fat.

"It's a mutual agreement," she continued. "God would bless and care for his people if they obeyed him."

Suddenly, that night at our 3–D Bible study, I saw myself in Jewish history, as one of the Israelites, admonished for forgetting the Lord's blessings. In the beginning of my Christian walk, I was so impassioned by this incredible love of Christ, that *yes, yes, of course I will follow you with my heart, body, and mind.*

How quickly good intentions wear off. When our own needs and desires take preference over the leading of the Holy Spirit.

I'm an attention lover, but I hate to get it by whimpers and sobs. I confessed it all, the whole shameful thing about Mike, which they suspected all along. And the curtain went up on my life story. I saw myself compared to the holiness of God. A demanding God who claims the right to be the center of our lives.

And for good reason. When we invite Christ to be the Lord of our life, we are striking a bargain with him, entering into a sacred handshake, one with no options. There are no prenuptials, no escape clause if we think we need it. You've heard of the golden handshake on the way out of a company? This is the *Golden Hello*, a pack of fringe benefits on the way into service, and it's all ours—the forgiveness, the peace and joy and strength.

And in a long-term relationship with the God of the universe.

Deuteronomy, I discovered, is one long plea for unshakeable obedience. In chapter 11, Moses urges the people to love God and keep his commandments. He tells them: Fear the Lord, walk in his ways, love and worship him *"with all your heart and all your soul"* (Deut. 11:13). If you obey, you'll have the *strength* to take over the land you're about to enter. And if you *carefully* obey, "I will provide rain for your land in season, the early and late rains, and you will harvest your grain, new wine, and oil" (Deut. 11:14).

"And have grass and fields for the livestock. Everything you could possibly need. You will eat and be satisfied. Be careful or you will be enticed to turn away."

How well I know about that.

"I set before you a blessing and a curse," Moses continued. "A blessing if you obey the Lord and a curse if you don't." Pretty clear-cut. Crops and harvest for doing it God's way, misfortune and calamity for choosing the opposite route.

We all know the verse in Jeremiah, "For I know the plans I have for you . . . plans for your welfare, not for disaster, to give you a future and a hope" (Jer. 29:11). So many times I received that Scripture scrawled in cards and encouraging notes after the locusts ruined my dreams, and it gave me boundless joy to think God cared enough to have plans for me. But the next line says it all: "You will call to Me and come and pray to Me, and I will listen to you. You will seek Me and find Me when you search for Me with all your heart."

All your heart. Holding nothing back. His plans for us are good, but they come with an even exchange, his favors for our faithfulness. "Keep the LORD's commands and statutes I am giving you today, for your own good" (Deut. 10:13).

Once we fully grasp this concept, our life can never be the same.

My friends never shook one finger at me in judgment for my indiscretion. "How can we help you?" they asked. "Help me to be obedient." From that day forward I pledged to walk in the light of the covenant relationship—God's way.

And the rewards were more than I imagined.

Years later I faced my first real crisis of faith, when Amy fled her troubled marriage. It's one thing to choose obedience to give up an immoral relationship, but Amy's situation was one of those gray areas.

Christian life is all about choices, and I was going to have to make one. In my own life the counselor's statement proved to be true: *Obedience is God's answer to your problem.* With Amy, I was not yet sure.

No matter what it takes, God's purpose
is to get us right with him.

revamp and renew

chapter 2

During those tense days when Amy was living with us, separated from Jesse, Carl saw a new side of me. "Jan—an attorney called for you today. A *family law* attorney."

Oops.

"She said you made an appointment for Amy?"

I threw back my shoulders. "Yes, I did."

"Honey, I understand how you feel as a mother," he said with diplomacy. "This must be so hard, but isn't it too soon to get involved? This isn't like you, not trusting God to work this out."

"God can't work this out. The marriage is over." I felt my heel grinding into the carpet. "And she needs to get on with her life!"

My husband gave me a sidelong look which meant: *What happened to the Jan I married?* A man of few words, he paused. Where was the Jan who first attracted him, the woman he admired, the one who urged people to hold the high ground, to persevere through the trials, believing, trusting, hoping, and waiting on the Lord? The woman he grew to love because she was a "strong woman of God"?

I gave him the *don't bug me now, can't you see I'm having a crisis* stare. How could he ever understand this? He didn't know my children as youngsters or see how they suffered with rejection from a man they worshipped. He wasn't there! Certainly, Amy made her bed getting into this marriage, but hasn't she had consequences enough? Does she have to be miserable the rest of her life?

I ached at the thought.

Except for loving pats every now and then, Carl avoided me the next few days. One morning he handed me the newspaper. "An interesting article from the *Sacramento Bee* you might enjoy." An article with a purpose—I can always count on that from Carl.

I'd left my legislative aide job at the state capitol a short time back but still kept up on all the battles in the legislature, so I devoured this piece. One of the members was in a political pickle for constantly siding with the "other party." Finally, he did the unthinkable—cast the dreaded swing vote on the budget. It angered his colleagues enough that they unanimously kicked him out of all caucus meetings.

The article dubbed the guy a *mugwump,* a person who acts independently—wavers and wobbles—and the phrase was coined in 1884 when a neutral Republican bolted from his party.

Hold it—are you inferring—? This isn't exactly a bolting from the faith thing, I started to argue. A fraction of unsteadiness, maybe, I admit to that.

OK, more than a fraction.

I could no longer see clearly from my perspective. Finally, I prayed, *Lord, help me see through this muddle.*

Does the Lord ever do this to you? Send you back through a medley of memories, a grab bag of your past? Looking back this way has benefit when it brings clarity to a muddy situation, when you scan the reruns of God's trustworthiness.

This was my Moses moment, a review of God's faithfulness in my daughter's life.

The scene: Amy, seventeen and pregnant—searching for love in all the wrong places—hurt, lost, and confused. Looking once more to her mother for guidance, a mother who wondered, after struggling as a single parent with two testy teenage girls, *Can it get any worse?*

Neither of my daughters responded to my firm hand and free advice. It usually meant packed suitcases. So this time I tried a different strategy. "What are you going to do?"

"Place the baby for adoption," she answered with certainty. The best thing for the child, I concurred. The logical best thing to do.

If only I wouldn't think of it as my grandchild.

"Will you help me select the adoptive family?" she asked, and we started the process at the local pregnancy center, viewing profile packets at home, choosing a couple to love this child. Things went along fine until the ultrasound, when we saw the baby girl blooming inside Amy. Then it hit me—another good-bye, another loss, and approaching very soon. But my heart assured me it was the right thing.

Not for every mother's pregnant daughter, but for mine.

At the end of her pregnancy, Amy panicked. "I can't do it. I can't give her up! I won't!" She called the adoptive parents and canceled the deal.

"Help me, Mom," she pleaded a few days later. "I'll go on welfare at first, live here, then find a job. I can do it if you help me."

My prodigal daughter is home at last, asking for my help. Talk about wrestling. Me and God in heart-to-heart combat for several nights.

Lord, I can't stand to see Amy this way. She's suffered so much, she's lost so much. Maybe there's another way. I can help her support this baby, help raise her. Maybe having a baby will grow Amy up and bring her back to me.

But the piercing truth remained: Amy was too fragile, too scarred, and not ready. *Adoption is best for this baby.*

Finally, I rustled up the courage. "Amy, I love you. I want what's right for you, but she's your responsibility. I'll support whatever decision you make, but if you want to keep her, you'll have to figure out a way to make this work."

I cringed. *She may hate me. She'll probably run away again. I'll lose my girl one more time.*

And yes, she hated me, but she stayed home and cast a very cold shoulder. We tiptoed around each other for weeks, and then labor started.

With her older sister Jenny and me at her side, Amy delivered a precious little girl. Then I sprinted from the room, stifling my tears. *Lord, why does it have to be so hard?* The next morning, two friends came over unannounced, a gift from God to prop me up in my weakness. After a steaming cup of tea, we prayed for the situation, praying in God's will for the *right thing.*

In the midst of prayer, the phone jingled. "Mom," Amy gasped, "the baby's in an incubator. Something's wrong with her. Oh, Mom—is she being punished for what I've done?"

"No, sweetheart—no. Jeanne and Sandra are here, and we'll pray for her right this minute."

"I've been wrestling all night. I've called the adoptive parents—to give them the baby. I know I have to make good on my promise."

Clenched fist to my pulsating chest, I thought of the verse I almost gave Amy hoping she'd come to her senses: "The Lord demands that you promptly fulfill your vows . . . for . . . you have vowed to the Lord your God" (Deut. 23:21, 23 TLB).

Because Amy was a Christian—she accepted the Lord at twelve and rededicated her life at a midnight baptism at Christian Encounter Ranch several years later—she could find no peace about the *wrong* decision.

That night, the doctors announced the baby would be—miraculously—fine.

Did God bring on the baby's mystery illness? When facing the unexplainable, I don't ponder those things anymore. Clearly, he used the momentary crisis with the baby to speak to Amy's heart, to assure her he was there, that she could keep her promise and trust him with the results.

One glitch in the mix: she insisted on bringing the baby home for a week. "I need time to say good-bye."

This is a way of letting go? Holding and feeding your baby all week? She needed to hold her, sing to her, write a loving letter. Yet I could not get too close. *Don't let me bond with this child, Lord.* While Amy spent bittersweet hours with her baby, I got familiar with the mall.

When the going gets tough, the tough go shopping.

The next weekend we invited friends and family on both sides for an adoption ceremony. Amy asked Mike, her counselor at the ranch for troubled teens where she spent eight months, to officiate. Emotionally drained, I had no energy to cook and bought appetizer trays from the market, but nobody ate very much.

Nikki's adoptive parents and new grandmother were eager to see their baby. Mike read passages from the book of 1 Samuel. "Hannah was childless, considered a failure in Old Testament times. She poured her soul out to the Lord and made a vow; if God would remember her and grant her a son, she would give him to the Lord for all the days of his life."

God opened her womb and granted her heart's desire, and when it was time, she followed through on her promise; she dedicated Samuel to the Lord's service. "Hannah gave up what she wanted most in the world," Mike added. "It was a gift, a gift that cost her everything."

It was grab and dab as hands flew to the tissue boxes to attend to moist eyes.

"She returned him to the God who had given him to her," Mike said. "Little did Hannah know that her son would be a mighty prophet of the Lord and anoint the first two kings of Israel."

A vow is a sacred thing to God. Like Hannah, Amy followed through on her promise, trusting that someday she would understand that the greatest joy in having a child is giving her freely back to God.

And like Hannah, she would trust in the yet unseen blessings, the words of God that promised, "I will honor those who honor Me" (1 Sam. 2:30). That someday he would use her to help heal other unmarried pregnant girls.

The happy ending tarried quite a while. Amy still struggled, not with her decision—she seldom looked back—but with her inner demons, her anger and guilt over the mistakes and wasted years. And there was nothing a mother could do; the battle was Amy's alone.

Once the family moved across country, it took years before I could crack a smile at a baby in pink and not swallow back the tears.

Then one day, after Nikki turned five, the family came to California to visit relatives, and they asked me to meet them at the zoo. After a playful afternoon of hide-and-seek and feeding the ducks, her grandmother Grace said to me, "She's such a special child, such a blessing to me. *Thank you*, Jan."

She thanked me because Nikki was a gift from God that came through me. With my stinging tears, I finally understood what Mike said that night—our sacrifice of obedience—difficult as it is—becomes a wellspring of blessing for others.

This memory at my kitchen table led to a train of thought without a caboose. God's hand was on Amy. Despite the flashbacks I still staggered between my beliefs and my desires. Amy deserved to be happy. If only I could trade places with my daughter. Let me plod through a painful marriage. I've done the long-suffering wife and worn the mask of making the best of a foolish marital decision.

When it comes to seeing our children in anguish, it's easy to slip into temporary insanity. When the truth takes on a maternal or paternal haze, it can bring on a batch of blind spots.

I knew what Carl would say about Amy giving Jesse another chance, so why bother kibitzing with him about it? *We all have our cross to bear, honey. You'll get in the way of God's work if you try to bear it for her. Let him go to work to heal this marriage.*

But what if he doesn't?

Then, in his sweet and gentle way, Carl would remind me what taking up our cross really means—following our Lord *even in our suffering.* He'd quote me his favorite verse, Philippians 3:10: "My goal is to know him and the *power* of His resurrection." Then remind me again of the words we omit from memory, "and the *fellowship* of His sufferings, being conformed to His death" (author's emphases).

Obedience often hurts.

Another one of Carl's pet lines: "Obedience either applies all the way across our lives or it doesn't."

Ouch. How true it is.

With a giant deflating sigh I plopped myself on the futon in our sunroom and watched the Casablanca fan spin hot air from the ceiling. I thought of our *Experiencing God* Bible study, the first fellowship opportunity at our new church shortly after we got married. *Experiencing God: Knowing and Doing the Will of God.*

Author Henry Blackaby talks about a crisis of belief. *It comes when God leads you into a God-sized decision and you question it.*[1] In the workbook, the examples refer to ministry opportunities, when God wants to do something through us and we resist, but we often face judgment calls like mine with Amy.

I was forging full steam ahead with what I considered noble plans for my daughter, a new start, with me footing the entire bill. Worthy motives born of love, and yet I knew what God's Word says about marriage being a lifetime commitment. As a rejected spouse of an unbeliever who left me for greener pastures, I spent a fair amount of time boning up on this whole divorce and remarriage subject.

I know where God stands on marriage when both are believers—stay in it (1 Cor. 7). And that's no suggestion, but a *command*. I've seen this raise some hairs on the back of many stiff necks: What about *this* circumstance? What about *that?* There are cases where a marriage cannot be saved and the line must be drawn, but when it comes to a sincere, repentant partner, I always say, "Hang in there."

Welcome to your crisis of belief, Jan. The place where you feel the pinch. It's the turning point, according to Blackaby, your personal hour of decision. *What you do next reveals what you really believe about God.*

Yikes.

Under pressure, faced with tests and challenges, our faith is forced into the open, and our true colors come out.

Yikes again.

Did I believe God had a purpose for a miserable marriage? That he was a God of impossible situations? That he could work out a big mess and use it for his glory?

Yes. Then why did I find it so difficult to trust Amy to her heavenly Father? I'd had lots of practice, so many times in her prodigal years. Instead, I was subtly encouraging her—with a bit of plotting and planning—to cut all the ties and walk away without giving God a chance to work.

As if he'd get it wrong.

It was a decision that seemed so right in my eyes.

Truth: I resented her living in Southern California and wanted her to be close by, to make up for the years spent apart. Yet she had a husband, whom I didn't like very much, and a little son, whom I adored.

What God has joined together . . . let no man—or woman . . .

Remember the Sermon on the Mount that begins with "Blessed are those . . ."? Even a quick read through will remind us of what those three chapters—Matthew 5, 6, and 7—are about, the "new" way, how Christ followers should live, not the "old" way of the religious scribes and Pharisees.

The new covenant versus the old one.

Jesus tells us to enter (the kingdom) through the narrow gate, the road that leads to life (Matt. 7:13). It's a single-track road, barely enough room for one pair of boots. It's so narrow you get pinched and squished and scraped. *And only a few find it.*

The obedient few.

Pondering it all that morning, the answer was as clear as the view of Sacramento from my hilltop deck on a rare smogless day; I must make every effort to support this couple in restoring the relationship. Dust off the old pom-poms and root for reconciliation.

Maybe there will be no more divorces in this family.

"When God speaks to you, revealing what he is about to do, that revelation is your invitation to adjust your life to him," Blackaby writes.[2] *Adjustments prepare you for obedience.* And the greatest single difficulty in following God may come at the point of adjustment.[3]

When you must be totally dependent on God to work through you and in you.

As Carl shared from his morning devotional, "Our goal is not to try to be a good Christian. Our goal is total dependence on God moment by moment."

Lord, help me stand firm for what's right. Help me trust you moment by moment with my daughter.

There is only one real choice when facing difficult times—to stand on faith and act on what we know and trust. God had his hand on Amy, that I knew, and through her life story would bring honor to himself. And he didn't need me as a coauthor, editing the script to my satisfaction.

I will tear up the lawyer's phone number and invite Jesse to fly up for the weekend.

I straightened up from my slouch and flung off a throw pillow. A meager chuckle escaped from my mouth. I would stand firm *with purpose*. God's wonderful, divine purpose. No mug-wumping for me. No juicy stories about Jan Coleman in *God's Daily Gazette*. Banned from the party because she's wishy-washy in her faith.

OK, so I slipped a bit—we all do—but I'm back on track now. Back on the road that may be steep, narrow, and bloody, but the only one with the true light of truth at the end.

Hebrews 12:28 sums it up for me. "Therefore, since we are receiving a kingdom that cannot be shaken, let us hold on to grace. By it, we may serve God acceptably, with reverence and awe."

An unshakeable Christian, that's my goal, one with a steadfast heart of obedience.

Devoted to God, anchored to his truth, tethered to his ways. Determined to follow him *no matter what*.

That's what this book is all about: Loving God with all your heart and with all your soul and with all your strength so you can do as he wishes and reap the rewards. There are stories from all situations and many crises of faith, most of which I've witnessed.

Proverbs says that the righteous will never be uprooted. Think of it—no matter what tornado stirs through life, your heart is fixed, your feet squarely planted, your future secure.

There is a cost to following God, but it's only a temporary discomfort, and it's pale compared to the perks, growing into a person beyond doubt, beyond reproach—one who is, as my political pals would say, unimpeachable.

When it comes to doing the right thing,

we have to get on God's side of the debate.

And the results are not up to us.

those who honor me

chapter 3

We drove Amy back home to her husband in Southern California. "It's going to be OK," she repeated at least a dozen times while switching between country music stations. Then the awkward greeting at her front door, the apprehension behind the smile, our swift good-byes—they didn't need us hanging around—and my feeling that I'd just set my baby adrift in a reed basket on the river.

Years ago a friend pointed out that I was joined at the hip with Amy. "You've got to cut the umbilical cord, for both your sakes," she said. Yeah. Yeah. I know. But somehow I'd always gather my lost chick back under my wing. I'm a mom after all. At that moment, driving away from her house, I saw what severing that tie really meant.

Giving her future to God, once and for all. When Hannah left her young son at the tabernacle, she said, "As sure as you live, my lord, I am the woman who stood here beside you praying to the LORD. I prayed for this boy, and since the LORD gave me what I asked Him for, I now give the boy to the LORD. For as long as he lives, he is given to the LORD" (1 Sam. 1:26–28).

The Lord had given *me* what I asked for. He had not let go of Amy. He had wooed her heart back to him. Now he was about to go to work restoring her life in his way, in his time, and my job was to praise him for it the way Hannah did. "There is no one holy like the LORD; There is no one besides you; There is no Rock like our God" (1 Sam. 2:2 NIV).

The next few months I watched her struggle to ignite the smallest spark of love for Jesse. He tried to be a good husband, and though he stopped lashing out physically, he wasn't coping well in the readjustment stage. His temper still flared; they still argued bitterly. But she didn't cower anymore; she stood her ground.

And stayed the course, devoted to the Lord. Firm and undaunted. She refused to rock on the porch of regret. She sought her identity and self-worth through Jesus alone.

Yet, in her secret moments, my daughter wondered if this would be her destiny, just making do with her mess. I wondered, *In the same situation could I do this?* "Mom, I *know* I couldn't," her sister Jennifer said. To us Amy was a brave little soldier and deserved a Purple Heart.

"God will reward your faithfulness," I told her with forced confidence. And in my prayers I cried, *Lord, don't make me a liar.*

The next summer the family drove up to our mountain cabin for their vacation. Four days later the phone rang. "Mom, I've had it. It's over. I sent Jesse home. Will you come get me?"

Huh? Where did I bury that umbilical cord? Her sister Jenny came to the rescue. "I'll go, Mom. We need some sister time any-way." When Amy and her toddler finally got to my house, I had a hold of my runaway perspective and set it right. It was her life, her choice. And difficult for everybody, especially her son. But this time my heart throbbed in pain for how God must be grieving. My thoughts were on him.

What a switch.

"I've got to go home and take care of things," she said. "But I'm coming up here to live and start over. I'll make it on my own." So off again we went to Southern California. Stuck in a traffic jam on the Grapevine before heading into the Los Angeles basin, I listened to her explanation of why things had deteriorated. But this time Mom didn't rag on Jesse. This time she saw it differently. Amy had grown impatient with trusting God; he wasn't moving fast enough to give her the marriage she envisioned. So she took it in her own hands again.

And this time Mom was hands-off.

For six tense weeks they were separated. Then Amy discovered she was pregnant. Oops. From one of their brief passionate moments between skirmishes.

As it says in Proverbs 19:21: Many plans are in a man's heart, but the LORD's decree will prevail.

In the next few months, hemmed in again by God, my daughter began to see her own wrong responses—her unrealistic expectations, the pressure she unknowingly put on Jesse—and the couple came to a truce.

Fast-forward to the birth of their second son and guilty tears as she wondered, "Couldn't you have given me a daughter, Lord? I gave mine up for you."

Let it go and trust me.

And she did. Focusing on her own obedience, not her husband's performance, love began to sprout from unexpected corners of Amy's heart. As she learned to respect Jesse's strengths, he grew more tender and responsive. It is now four years later, and he's a leader in church and at home. The relationship wasn't rebuilt—its original parts were faulty—it was reformed from two willing hearts.

"I've been looking for something all my life," Amy claims, "but it's not to be found; it must be made." And the ingredients start with willingness.

And just when she'd gotten used to planes, trucks, and boisterous boys—"two is quite enough, and Jesse is going in for a vasectomy," she declared—a pregnancy test came back positive again. "This time I know it's a girl. God is giving me my girl."

And he did; little Carly arrived two years ago. *I will honor those who honor Me.*

What if my plans for the dissolution of Amy's marriage had succeeded? What would my pure motives have produced—a new start for my daughter, but at what price? We can't guess at the outcome, but I do know this: God's way proved far better than mine. At best Amy would have been neatly divorced and Andrew settled in a nice Christian school with happy grandparents as spectators at all the pageants and events.

But he would still be the product of a broken home, one I helped destroy.

Proverbs tells children: "Listen . . . to your father's instruction, and don't reject your mother's teaching, for they will be a garland of grace on your head" (Prov. 1:8–9).

Good advice as long as parents seek wisdom. I considered my view of Amy's dilemma quite balanced; ending a disastrous marriage is not so unusual, and Andrew would be better off in a more positive situation. But this is the world's wisdom and not the Lord's. Paul told the Corinthians, "For it is written, 'I will destroy the wisdom of the wise, and I will set aside the understanding of the experts'" (1 Cor. 1:19).

A theme that keeps tracking like an escalator in our adult Sunday school class: "Do you worship God or your own opinions?" our teacher asks. Soft spoken and inoffensive, Hal can get away challenging us like a prophet. He teaches strictly from God's Word. The thirty or so who show up every week come with spiritual shovels to dig into the truth.

Last month, before Hal went out of town, he called on his "dream team" to continue our unfinished discussion of Matthew 5.

We'd been clipping along through this Gospel until we hit the verses on divorce. Two Sundays later we were still chewing on it, commenting on how we live in "no-fault divorce" land, and how divorce is only a mouse click away with the do-it-yourself Web site.

Did it hit too close to home for some in the group? Did they wonder: *Are we bordering on legalism here or what? Isn't this a "to each his own" issue?* And some of the wounds were still too fresh.

Somebody shared from an article on a new concept called "covenant marriage" spearheaded by Dennis Rainey, founder of the "I Still Do" conferences.[1] Couples can agree to tougher restrictions on dissolving their marriage—counseling first for instance—and the document becomes a sacred covenant instead of a civil arrangement.

They're opting to make it harder to end the relationship, to give God a chance to work. Such a novel idea.

The class was just getting warmed up when the edgy issue of remarriage surfaced. "Wrap it up while I'm gone," Hal said. "Some people are staying away because of the subject matter."

See my jaw drop. I found this hard to swallow. According to the Barna Group, more than a third of so-called "born again" believers have gone through a divorce. It affects—and infects—us all at some point. Isn't it best for all Christians to be more informed and armed with ways to support a struggling marriage?

Then God reminded me of my former viewpoint on the divorced, before I was one—misfits, odd ducks, and flawed somehow. Few families experienced divorce when I grew up, and my marriage failed in a small town where it was not common to live unmarried.

As a volunteer on the "dream team," I came prepared the following week, not armed with an abundance of Scriptures but with powerful stories of a God who, despite the hopeless evidence, can and does restore. Amy and Jesse are proof of it.

My neighbor Amara is in our class, and she and Wayne are a happily remarried couple. "But I want my children to know the horror of divorce," she said. "When my first husband and I divorced, nobody tried to stop us, to convince us to give it a second look. If the same thing happens to my children, I'll get right in their face with the truth!"

We may have been discussing marriage and the disaster of divorce in our class, but the principles are universal and timeless. Jesus surrendered control of himself wholly to God. It's what he prepared his whole life to do, to commit himself to the Father's hands. "He humbled Himself by becoming obedient to the point of death—even to death on a cross. For this reason God also highly exalted Him and gave Him the name that is above every name" (Phil. 2:8–9).

God has a blanket will for all of us—in marriage, in singleness, as parents—and we learn it from the Bible, but there are specific applications, unique to each of us, that only the Holy Spirit can teach.

And the light to live by glows in the deep regions of an obedient heart.

Robert Ashcroft, former pastor and college president—and father of U.S. Attorney General John Ashcroft who credits his father with teaching him the moral values that shaped his life—once said, "All of heaven is waiting to help those who will discover the will of God and do it."

I thank heaven for helping me.

There's always a price to pay for
choosing God's way.

crossing the rubicon— no turning back

chapter 4

Moses told the Hebrews, "This command that I give you today is certainly not too difficult or beyond your reach" (Deut. 30:11).

But sometimes it's a very long reach.

Our associate pastor Tim wears many hats in our fast-growing church—counselor to the confused, overseer of small groups, author of our studies on the Sunday sermon, relief preacher, computer guru, doughnut provider, and parking lot attendant when necessary. He's cooperative, adaptable, and his respectful smile is a warm welcome every Sunday morning.

When he answered his call to the ministry, Tim faced his critical moment, when he had to cross the Rubicon. A trail that would lead him away from his family.

"*Crossing the Rubicon*" is a familiar phrase to those of us who live near Georgetown, California, where they hold the annual

Jeepers Jamboree. If you have a four-wheel drive and are mildly insane, you can brave the famous Rubicon Trail that winds its way up to Tahoe.

Thousands flock from around the world to do this.

The phrase "crossing the Rubicon" actually means to take *decisive action* from which there is no turning back.

The Jeepers borrowed it from ancient Roman law when generals were forbidden from crossing the Rubicon River to enter Italy. When Julius Caesar ignored the command in 49 BC, it started a bloody civil war.

Tim's decision to enter the ministry almost did the same.

A military family, the Gregorys, were devout Catholics. With no fixed address for very long, Tim grew up with no roots. As a teenager, he felt restless and began exploring answers to spiritual questions. "First I approached the priests, but they couldn't help me get a handle on what was missing in my soul. I knew there had to be more."

Some guys from a local youth group invited him to play football, and he saw a difference in them. "They liked church and attended Bible studies. I tagged along with them, and a few months later became a believer."

The day of his baptism was unsettling for Tim's mother. "I can't see why it's necessary. You were already baptized."

"It strained our relationship," Tim says. Once in college, he and his dad had lively discussions on his visits home about church and religion. After a few summer mission trips, Tim sensed a pull toward full-time ministry. "In my junior year I had a strong sense that God wanted me to do this with my life."

But for a year he wrestled. "Is this really from the Lord? And what will my life look like? Nothing resembling my parents' dreams for their son. They were footing the bill for college, and the time came to let them in on my plans so they would know the direction I was heading."

It kicked his dad out of gear. Angry, he tried to steer his son back to reality. "You're throwing away your life!" It was the early eighties, in the midst of the Jim Jones People's Temple era. Was something sinister controlling his son's mind, he wondered? Was he involved in one of those killer cults? It made no earthly sense.

God's ways seldom do.

"We're not supporting you anymore," he told Tim. "You're on your own."

Suddenly they cut Tim off, financially and emotionally. "The day I packed up for seminary, my mom said good-bye, but my dad wouldn't speak to me. I could handle supporting myself through seminary. I could struggle to make ends meet and live on peanut butter and jelly sandwiches, but this decision had cost me closeness with my family."

And the love of his high school sweetheart, the woman he always thought he'd marry. "She had this inaccurate picture of what a pastor's wife should be, and I couldn't persuade her." She balked at the idea of this future with Tim. "I could never fulfill that," she confessed and broke off the relationship.

"This was my crisis of faith, the catalyst for choosing God's way no matter what. My choice cost me the woman I loved." Through long days and lonely nights of soul searching in the dorm room, Tim finally settled the question of where his loyalty lay. And he grasped the inescapable fact: following Christ may isolate you from those you love.

Jesus knew that we would face this conflict. "The person who loves father or mother more than Me is not worthy of Me; the person who loves son or daughter more than Me is not worthy of Me" (Matt. 10:37).

Christ would never urge us to revolt against our family, defy them for our own selfish wants, but his personal presence in our lives requires we sign a pledge on the dotted line. And it's always the better choice. "The kingdom of God is within us," Tim says, "and we are earmarked, set aside from the beginning to reflect God with our lives. Our purpose is written on our hearts. We choose to follow God, and we'll find that purpose."

Consider Moses. He must have felt like the Lone Ranger before teaming up with Tonto, leading the charge by himself for God. It's easy to enter heavenly active duty when there's a send-off rally at the train station. Only those with persistent faith can obey the call when the streets are silent and empty.

Setting out alone and unsupported takes courage.

"If you started analyzing the cost of obedience," Tim adds, "you wouldn't do it. If you did the debit/credit thing, the debits would be too high."

Tim and his newly saved sister became the object of shrugs and sneers, "Oh, you know, those *Baptists*." But their cousin, Mac, who joined up with the mob in L.A. won the family's affection like a charming movie pirate. "He was finally arrested, put up a million-dollar bond in cash, and then jumped bail. He's still locked up in federal prison."

Tim chuckles when he relates how the family kept pressing, "Did you send poor Mac a Christmas card?" While he and his sister were following God, "We were being treated like the black sheep of the family, and Mac was the darling of the clan."

Back at seminary, Tim pressed toward his goal. When he met Susan, their friendship grew into a serious romance. "God had orchestrated everything. He had kept me from settling for second best." He and Susan are a great complement to each other.

Eventually Tim's parents accepted his chosen career when he joined the Air Force Reserves. "God had been bringing people into my life over the years who would ask me if I'd ever thought about the chaplaincy. I kept brushing them off until one day it just clicked: that's what I was to do, be a military chaplain."

His dad did a turnaround. Being a pastor might not make sense to an ex-GI, but lifting the morale of the military sure does. Now Tim is a weekend warrior, "serving as a representative of the Holy," reminding soldiers there is a God who cares about them. "And there's closeness with my family again," he says.

As we chatted in his office, I asked Tim when you know if you've come to your Rubicon. "One thing: affirmation from other believers. You will question, *is the risk worth it?* But penetrating through the question will be friends who say, *I see God using you here.*"

When Moses talked about God's call, he expressed that it was not in the heavens or across the sea. "But the message is very near you, in your mouth and in your heart, so that you may follow it" (Deut. 30:14).

We all have our hour of decision. If the Lord is the core of your life, the *raison d'être*—your reason for existing—no matter how hot things get, he will be your constant heat shield.

He came through for Beth. She made a choice that brought about the end of her marriage. "You can't be pregnant," her husband responded when she broke the news, but they couldn't wish their child away; the test had come back positive.

"Then you'll just have to have an abortion," he insisted. "I'll take full responsibility for it."

And what does *that* mean, Beth wondered as she grappled with the bare facts; his plans didn't include starting over with a new baby, not with their two sons nearly teenagers. *He says he'll take responsibility, but I'm the one who will end the life of this child. I'm not keen about such a midlife pregnancy either, but what is the right thing to do?*

Beth had knocked herself out trying to please this man. She'd been counseled in the *obedient wife* school, so when he made an appointment at an abortion clinic, she didn't speak up and left the house in compliance. "On my way out of town, I stopped at the pay phone in front of Safeway and cancelled. Of course, they tried to talk me into keeping the appointment."

That night when she told Jim was a night she will not forget. "He said if I wouldn't get an abortion, he'd leave me. I knew then it was only an excuse. He'd probably leave me anyway."

For weeks she'd been reading books about abortion from a Christian perspective, seeking the truth revealed through the presence of God, a new concept for her. The traditional church of her youth had been a wonderful way to grow up—she'd sung in the choir and met Jim there—but it never addressed her hidden hunger for a oneness with the Lord, a hunger that mistakenly led her to place her husband on the throne of her life. A new friend counseled her, "Trust the Lord. This baby is supposed to be born."

She took hold of the promise, clutching like a toddler to a father's firm finger.

Jim did not leave as threatened but clammed up for months, going through the motions of fatherhood but remaining emotionally absent from Beth. When labor came, a friend drove her to the hospital; her husband didn't show up until hours later. "The nurse pushed our daughter into his arms that day, but he wouldn't touch or hold her for the first three months of her life."

Bring on the baby blues. Beth sank to the lowest point in her life. "I was distraught. I went batty," she admits. "I really thought they'd all be better off without me. I had messed it all up, ruined my husband's life. He blamed me for getting pregnant when we'd both agreed our family was complete. It was all my fault. I might as well kill myself and the baby."

Satan the deceiver had thrown dust in her eyes.

At the stove stirring a pot of oatmeal, Beth cried out to the Lord, *If I'm not supposed to take my life, show me.* "It was like one of those movie moments, accompanied by a sentimental melody. Instantly, a brilliant light shone through the window and warmed me to the bone—an amazing moment. I knew I was to give my whole heart to God, and he would not desert me through this."

It's what my friend and author Cecil Murphey calls the moment the "Relentless One" chooses to invade our life.[1] When we stop fighting. When he reaches down because we can't reach high enough to make the connection.

We call that grace.

Jim came in to pour his morning coffee, and she noticed his tense jaw, stubborn tears behind the determination. He was a man in turmoil, soon to make the worst decision of his life in the guise of "looking out for number one."

The dog-eared book currently on his nightstand, Jim consumed every word of it, the best selling example of the new wave of the 1980s, a call to stop blindly accepting the customs of society or the church and end the charade of living the expected selfless life—an invitation to disappointment and frustration. Scanning it one morning, Beth saw listed all the reasons why you shouldn't stay in a bad relationship *because of children*—the age-old lie that the kids will be worse off growing up with two unhappy parents.

A few months later Jim moved out. Beth had crossed her Rubicon, a spiritual milestone with no turning back, standing for what she knew was right, only to watch her childhood sweetheart take a pain-inflicting detour.

• • • •

Daniel's pals—Shadrach, Meschach, and Abednego—were determined to stand for God no matter what. Carried away to Babylon as teenagers, they were among the favored few, the crème de la crème of captives, now in training for King Nebuchadnezzar's service. Complete with new names to help them blend into the culture.

It would take more than losing their Hebrew identity to embrace the practices of this pagan place.

Daniel determined not to defile himself (Dan. 1:8), and his friends held fast with him, refusing to eat any unclean food offered to idols. In my earlier days I would have argued, "Oh, let's just give in. We have no choice; it's out of our hands."

We always have a choice but not usually the comfortable one.

Daniel's creativity saved the day—read about it in Daniel 1—and years later we see him as a sort of White House chief of staff with his companions as his top aides. Then the king comes up with a new scheme to unite the country in worship, bowing down to a giant gold statue.

Dare refuse and into the fiery furnace you go, says the king.

What a test for young men well versed in the Ten Commandments; they were not to worship idols. So these men gave thumbs-down, refusing the king, and he finally blew. "Blazing fire it is," the king says. And what god can rescue you from that?

"We don't need to give you an answer to this question," the fearless men answered. "If the God we serve exists, then He can rescue us from the furnace of blazing fire, and He can rescue us from the power of you, the king. But even if He does *not* rescue us, we want you as king to know that we will not serve your gods or worship the gold statue you set up" (Dan. 3:16–18).

OK, if that's how you want to play. "Then Nebuchadnezzar was filled with rage, and the expression on his face changed toward Shadrach, Meshach, and Abednego. He gave orders to heat the furnace seven times more than was customary" (Dan. 3:19).

You may know the story. The young men are completely untouched by the fire and heat. Pressured to deny God—like Tim and Beth—they stood firm, and God was glorified.

How many times do we approach God with an attitude of, "If you make it easy, I'll take that Jeep trip on the Rubicon. After all, it's risky and I might bang up my SUV or get shook up traversing those steep canyons and riverbeds. If you can't guarantee me a safe trip, I'll just have to find another way."

Come on, we've all been there. Somehow, we're under the assumption that God cares first about our comfort when he's more concerned about our character. It may be unpleasant, but he's positioning us for a purpose. I can't help but think of the remarkable story of Joseph, sold into slavery by his jealous brothers. From that disaster he rose to become the most powerful minister of Egypt and rescuer of his people. Joseph's life shows us that the Lord works through adversity.

Joseph, a most handsome man, found a position working for Potiphar, the captain of Pharoah's guard who noticed his integrity and promoted him to overseer. Then Potiphar's wife cast her eye on Joseph. "Come with me," she enticed. Joseph refused and ran from the house. But women love the last word, so she whisked off his white linen loincloth and used it as evidence: *Joseph defiled me.*

The enraged husband threw him in jail.

Punished for doing the right thing—how can this be of God? When we ask these questions, we focus on the negative, when there is always a deeper unknown reason. What I admire about Joseph is that he didn't waste time asking why but, "Now what?"

He made his first priority loving and pleasing God. Many of us can't relate to Joseph, who responded in the right way all the time, who impressed everyone he met, but we can connect to how his brothers betrayed and deserted him.

Beth sure can. The next decade was shaky for her. "I was really on the fence for a while, chasing self-acceptance, wondering if God had forgotten me. I assumed that because I chose him things would steadily improve for me, but those were hard years, and I strayed off course. Yet I knew he was there waiting for me to turn to him. I just had to work out a few things first, but it was a costly detour, I can tell you that. "

Me too. I watched it all from a distance.

Still she committed to having her fractured family in a Bible-believing church every Sunday. Jim had remarried, and his new wife's interest in the children grew stale in short order. "That's a kind statement at best," Beth adds. "My kids were basically fatherless, and the boys were often out of hand."

But Kristen flourished in Sunday school and came to know Christ when she was ten. "She inspired me," Beth said. "My hunger for God raged in full force." Mother and daughter were baptized together in a country pond. "I would be lukewarm no longer. That day marked the real beginning of my commitment, and it's been a steady uphill climb ever since, learning what a true love relationship is with the living God."

Kristen's brothers, with their toes in the world testing out its pleasures, were more than intrigued by their sister's commitment at such a young age. Several months later they followed suit and stepped over to God's side.

The whole family had finally crossed the Rubicon. "The Lord used that baby in a mighty way."

The secret of true obedience is a close and unmistakable personal relationship with God.

Tim and Beth are two that have it.

*We learn to trust God by
small steps of obedience.*

step-by-step
and single file

chapter 5

When Sheron's abusive husband left, there was no longer a family structure for her young son. "I searched the Scripture for counsel on how to bring him up alone. It says that God is the father to the fatherless, and a father is one you imitate and obey, so I made Jesus the head of our household."

Every evening for dinner an empty chair sat designated for God—the father and husband—and Sheron made certain every decision-making conversation included Christ's blueprint for living.

Like all adolescent boys, Tim "copped an attitude" toward parental authority. "If he hesitated to obey, insisting his perspective was correct," Sheron said, "I would send him to his room for a 'talk' with his father. It could be something like taking out the garbage, mowing the lawn, or wanting to go somewhere inappropriate. I'd say, 'I'm your mother, and I can tell you what to do, but why not have a heart-to-heart talk to your dad about this? Whatever you two decide is OK with me.'" Tim never once came out of his room without the desire to do the right thing, to be obedient to his mom.

Tim's father breezed in and out of his life through the years, but as a Mormon he disagreed with Tim's choice of a Christian college and disowned him completely. Unfair and cruel though it was, Tim counted less on his biological father's emotional or financial support in his youth than his spiritual father. God would provide—and he did, through scholarships and missionary discounts, and a minimal amount of student loans.

Sheron beams when she speaks of her son, a former teacher and coach at a Christian school in Hawaii, who is now a competence advisor and development consultant for a large oil company. A father of two, Tim now mentors small group leaders in a large church in Texas.

Grateful that he learned very young how to hear the voice of God.

Tim learned obedience one step at a time, and so did his mother. "As a single mom with a two-and-a-half-year old, I had little money and a new job. I had just rededicated my life to God and moved to Seattle, away from familiar negative surroundings. God challenged me to tithe. On bill-paying day, I said, *OK God, which one—insurance bill or tithe?* He answered *tithe.* I did—with much anxiety, fear, and trembling. During that month I received the amount for the insurance plus five dollars, a wink from God. That and many other small steps have brought me to a place where I can say I have never given anything to God that he hasn't given me something better in return—finances, circumstances, relationships, and my own personal healing issues."

My friend Russ can say the same. After a short-term missionary trip on a mercy ship, Russ caught a terminal case of evangelism fever, and the call on his heart was changing. To be certain he and God were on the same wavelength, Russ asked us—his counterparts in singles ministry—to join him in prayer about a major move; closing his contracting business to train with Youth With a Mission.

It was obvious that Russ needed to go.

When he finally wound his way to Mexico, it felt like home. His missionary efforts began to bear fruit, and then he met Sol. When Russ made an overseas call asking our opinion/approval on his forthcoming marriage—we'd been like family for several years—we didn't know what to say. Russ had been our spiritual leader, the Bible guru, the pastor/counselor of our motley crew. When he spoke, everybody listened. Surely, he was in tune with God on this one. Right?

"You know, Russ," I offered with all the authority I could muster. "Cross-cultural marriages come with a host of challenges, and she's quite a bit *younger* than you."

Infatuation clouded common sense. "I know, and I'm prepared. She's such a sweet, innocent woman, so pure and devoted to God, and we'll be ministering together."

Love is blind, but marriage is the eye-opener.

In traditional Mexican families the children stay home with parents until they marry. Sol was twenty-eight before she left the nest. She had prayed for a committed Christian, a rare breed in Mexico, and when she met this *gringo*, he was everything she could ask for.

As soon as the ink dried on the license, Sol started visiting her mother every day, and when apart, they would spend hours on the phone.

Her husband had now become Russ the Resentful. "There was no leaving and cleaving with Sol. It bordered on codependency. She looked to her mother first; my opinion wasn't necessary. It affected our relationship."

Two years later the marriage was a disaster—a fact obvious to me when he brought her to the States for a family visit, and they bunked at my house. With limited knowledge of English, Sol was shy and insecure with me, but she and Russ went at it in Spanish like two angry bees in a bottle. I didn't have to know the language; the prolonged snarls said it all.

The next summer they returned, and Sol had mastered a litany of English words, enough to confess her frustration. I listened intently as she fixed her favorite dish, pozzle, a hearty stew made with maize, pork, and chili.

Speechless, I hugged her and promised to pray.

The next morning she was on the phone in tears to her mother and asked my help in booking her a flight back home. "I'm leaving him."

Russ just shrugged his shoulders. "Oh, let her go."

Intervention time for Jan. "You can't give up on this marriage!" I shook my index finger at them like two naughty students. "Russ, you will blow your witness and your ministry, and all you've worked for. And Sol, didn't you tell me your aim is to please God with your life? You two have to work this out so God will be glorified. He is bigger than your problems."

A rubber-meets-the-road lesson going on here.

Disaster diverted, at least temporarily. When they returned south of the border, they met with the mission leader for relationship counseling. "They all agreed Sol was suffering from what is known in Mexico as *mamitas*," Russ explained. "The inability of a married woman to detach from her mother in a healthy way. Sol couldn't even loosen the apron strings, let alone cut them.

"Spending time with family came as second nature to me," she said. "Russ and I approached issues so differently. I needed interaction with my family. Yet all who counseled us agreed that I was the one with the problem. This did not set well with me at all."

One evening friends and relationship experts Don and Noreen showed up, and the conversation steered straight to the marriage problems. Like a seasoned prosecutor, Russ presented the damaging evidence and expected to be affirmed, but Don turned to him. "Reconciling the situation is more important than who is to blame. There is an unwilling spirit in you, and that's where you have to begin."

Come again? Russ almost ushered him right out the door but held his tongue and thanked him for the wise observation. "His statement seemed ridiculous, but I couldn't get it out of my mind. I looked up the word *reconcile*. It simply means 'making things right.'"

What was the Lord saying? "I wrestled with it for weeks. And finally, it hit me. I'd taken my role as head—*the head of every man is Christ and every woman is man*—to mean I was the lead, the trailblazer. My missionary goals—saving Mexico one heart at a time for Christ—took precedence. Sol, as my helpmate, should get her fulfillment from our work together. Her problems and adjustment issues were hers to resolve."

A slight miscalculation. The whole *unwilling spirit* thing nagged at him too. And he knew exactly what that was all about. Having a baby.

Before he popped the question years ago, Russ admitted to Sol that he had raised his family—after being divorced by his wife before he was a believer—and did not plan on a second round at fatherhood. "I was completely up-front with her. I did not want more children, so if she did, I was not her man. I was blameless on this one."

How could she pass up on such a godly man, Sol wondered? *Especially since he looks so much like Robert Redford.* Love-struck, she agreed to live with it; there would be no kids. Traveling and ministering as a couple would be enough.

A more than slight miscalculation. Shortly after the honeymoon she announced to her husband she desperately wanted a baby. "Let's just get a cat," Russ offered. Bristling at his attempt at wit, Sol replied, "I want a child. I'm a woman. I'm made that way."

"I felt betrayed." Russ said. "She lied to me."

That explains their fighting like bees in a bottle at my house.

Sol confirmed this as their major roadblock on their second visit. "I meant it when we married, that I could live without children, but I never knew how much I'd yearn to be a mother." She pressed at her waist. "I ache inside."

"We fought over this issue for the first five years," Russ said. "And God finally had his way with me. He was clearly calling me to *give in*. None of my 'what ifs' stood up against his 'just do its,' and then nothing seemed to be going right in my life—my marriage or my ministry. It was a painful holding pattern. Could it be connected to my resistance? So I relented about the baby, as much as I dreaded the idea. After all, I'd raised my kids already. It would mean an adjustment of my dreams of a traveling missionary. Yet, because God clearly willed it, I stopped questioning. And when Sol saw that I valued her and considered her needs, we both began to change. A spirit of contention between us gave way to graceful cooperation, and a greater understanding of God."

From one hesitant step of Spirit-led obedience.

"Clear as glass, I finally saw the truth," Russ said. "Until that point I had been selfishly thinking of me, and it was then that I truly began to love Sol. I took the love that Christ has for us and applied it to my own life in a way that *really cost me something*. I died to myself and my need to be free in order to see the life of my beloved fulfilled. I would honor and bless Sol with her heart's desire, *if I could.*"

And that was a big *if*. It meant a miracle surgery. Russ put his researching skills to work and found a Christian doctor in the States who was not only willing to perform the "replumbing" as he calls it, but for a very reasonable fee, as a ministry to couples.

Yet the doctor was less than optimistic. "Since it had been

twenty years since my vasectomy, we should expect five to six years before any viable sperms emerge."

Whoops. How about getting pregnant the second month?

"A true sign from God," added Russ.

In fairness, marriage for them is still a challenge at times. "And having a young daughter at my age is limiting in some respects but a bigger payoff than I imagined. She is a delight to me, and a child opens so many doors of communication with unbelievers," Russ says. "God knows best. I made the right choice, no regrets. If we seek and act on God's guidance, whether we feel like it or not, the postscript reads: *Big blessings in store.*"

Since their daughter Madison arrived, Russ and Sol found a new God-inspired vision, to plant house churches modeled after the first-century church in Acts: no buildings, sound systems, or paid staff, just groups of twelve to fifteen people who meet for worship, fellowship, and to eat together in their homes. Russ and Sol are pioneers in presenting this concept in Mexico, strategizing with others to find and draw together a network. Russ hopes to see this become a nationwide movement.

Russ is a trailblazer after all. "Christianity began with small steps; that's how God builds a kingdom."

The kingdom is what our counselor friend Ken discussed with me recently. He agreed to meet with me one morning at LaBou Café, my second office. When I blew through the door a few minutes late, I found him kicked back in a corner booth sipping a tall coffee and perusing the newspaper. "Just chill. I'm in no hurry this morning. So what's up?"

"I'm writing this book, and you are the reason, Ken." He peered at me from the rim of his glasses. I reeled off how Carl came back from the elders' meeting impassioned about Ken's presentation. "He mentioned your practice of sending clients to walk the grounds at the Weimar Institute. Can you tell me more about this?"

A grin crept up one side of his face. "When people come to me, it's a preemptive strike. What they've been doing no longer works, and they have no other options. I was at a boat show last weekend, and an old sailor there said something profound. 'We navigate up the rivers we know how to navigate.' Isn't that the way it is?"

He digressed on that story for a minute and then commented on his clients, "Their souls are not content, but they don't know that yet. The crisis that brought them to counseling blows open the discontent. It's the soul talking: 'I've got a life God wants me to live, but I don't know how.'"

Our lives are written on our hearts, Ken explained. "That's the kingdom Jesus spoke of."

You may recall that after the crucifixion, the apostles fled Jerusalem to ponder the *now what* question. When the resurrected Christ appeared, he told them to go into the world and preach the gospel, baptizing and teaching them to obey. "And remember, I am with you to the end of the age," Jesus said.

Hope renewed, it marked a new and glorious start. Acts tells us the rest of the story, how the disciples had been curious about the kingdom, when it would come and what part they would play in it. To the traditional Jew the Messiah was to come as a liberator, an Abraham Lincoln-type hero who would release them from years of Roman domination.

They never expected the Messiah to be captured and killed. What a shock.

Their first question to the risen Lord: "Are you restoring the kingdom to Israel?"

"Forget all that for now," he urged. We're talking about a spiritual kingdom here. Founded in the hearts of believers.

This small band of men became the kernel of a new community.

Jesus spoke about the kingdom more than any other topic, sixteen inches of Scripture references in the back of my study

Bible. "Seek first the kingdom of God" (Matt. 6:33), and "My kingdom is not of this world" (John 18:36).

"Most Christians haven't gotten the kingdom thing straightened out yet," Ken said. "We want to control our little worlds, but it leads to a life of total frustration."

When our hearts are living outside the reign of the kingdom of God.

That's why modifying behavior never works, Ken says. While Russ was grudgingly willing to help Sol have her baby, it was not until his heart understood the sacrifice, from a God's eye view, that it started to change. This is what kingdom living is all about. Doing the right thing for Sol was like a nuclear blast for his ministry. He wasn't giving up freedom; he was gaining it through the abundant life they would have as a family.

Ken discovered this concept through a Renovaré conference, based on a word meaning "spiritual renewal." At Ken's suggestion Carl and I attended a regional conference a few years ago, and Carl urged his elder board members to tag along the next year, to check out truths as old as olive trees. In our hectic world, being like and thinking like Jesus is something that does not come easy.

It starts with transforming the heart, one beat at a time. Everything we experience—job, family, books, films, and hobbies—shapes our spiritual life. We can choose to practice disciplines like study, worship, prayer, and solitude, and our spirits will be shaped for the good. The dark and dangerous lose their attraction as our spirits are fashioned into the image of Christ.[1]

Advice is not what you come to Ken for. "What I'm about is helping people do what they need to do to line up their lives with the King."

"And what's this strolling through the gardens of the Weimar Institute all about?" I asked him.

He grinned. "I send them up there for four hours a day for thirty days, with nothing, no Bible, no notebook. To be alone without distraction. Most people have their heads so filled with stuff, they wouldn't know what the kingdom of God was if it hit them in the face. In the solitude, they hear God's voice."

And how many actually make it thirty days, I asked?

"Nobody ever does it, but after two or three days, they begin to see what they are missing. Their problem is not the marriage relationship or the wayward kid or the job they hate or their addiction; it's that they have failed to connect with God, to understand his character. They need to discover why they were created: to fellowship with and serve God with the passions he gave them. Once they get that straight, they can give up control. They don't need to look to others to meet their needs or place blame. Their expectations fade away as pleasing God becomes their primary focus."

Seek first the kingdom of God.

So simple, yet we make it so difficult. Give God time in silence before him, to receive him through the Spirit, to sense his presence and power working in us, teaching us truth that we embrace with eagerness.

"Obeying God will never make sense unless it is in the context of the kingdom," Ken said. "We no longer see it as falling in line, but falling in love—with Christ."

I underlined that one and marked it with two big stars.

"When clients fail to hear God's voice, it's because *they don't want to*," Ken added with a sigh. "I wish these folks well and send them on their way."

As I skipped out to my car like Dorothy on the Yellow Brick Road, observers may have wondered if I had a triple shot of cappuccino. Instant invigoration, with a reminder from God that this too is my pursuit, to live the kingdom life. It's here with us and in us, and we are to spend our days reflecting it.

As Dietrich Bonhoeffer said: "One act of obedience is worth a hundred sermons."[2]

*Obedience is the formula for bringing
beauty out of ashes.*

new life in dry bones

chapter 6

Elaine pretended happiness for a long time. "My husband and I had two beautiful daughters and a nice house, but while I raised the kids, Brad buried himself in work and golf. I started to feel restless, searching for something more."

It was waiting at her local church, but she took a slight detour to find it.

"The veneer of what I thought was happiness began to peel off. My marriage was a sham. We were numb and disconnected from each other, two single people in the same house. There had to be more to life than that."

In a lively, growing community church in town, she sought out Christ, dove into his Word, connected with his people, and new life began to stir in her paralyzed heart. As the months passed, Elaine discovered her gifts through the worship ministry. "I felt special, needed, awakened to my value as a person for the first time."

She got hooked. Church became her solace and her salvation.

But it only added more fractures to a splintering marriage. Brad resisted any talk of spiritual things. "He became more emotionally distant and verbally abusive. We were at war daily. It was a miserable family life. I wondered, *How do I find joy? I can't even find forgiveness for this man.* I told the Lord, '*I can't do this anymore.*'"

Enter Satan the destroyer with a grand plan for murdering the marriage.

When Elaine was invited to attend a leadership conference that fall, she thought, *What a special privilege,* and went on the weekend with eagerness. Late one night she found herself in a deep conversation with the worship leader. "I listened to Dale share his pain and frustration over a broken relationship, and I felt myself longing to fix it. Soon I was opening up about my angry, unbelieving husband and our loveless marriage."

Close encounters of the dangerous kind.

"We revealed our intimate yearnings, and it happened so fast. The attraction was so strong. I saw him as my knight in shining armor appearing out of heaven to rescue me from my pain. He was a prize package—good looking, a professional man, dedicated to God and ministry. We could talk about the Bible for hours. And he was raising his kids, hands-on involved with them, while Brad was failing as a parent in my eyes."

All the ingredients were there—for an upside-down cake destined to flop.

"The more we tried to back off, the more intense were the feelings. We crossed the line, sharing too many intimate things. We were in over our heads. He valued me, understood my love for the arts, and wanted to support my growth. In contrast, Brad resented the time I spent on my art and criticized me for the time I spent in ministry, taking time away from his selfish needs. Meanwhile Dale promised me the marriage of my childhood dreams. He wanted to nurture me, take care of me, share ministry with me."

An appetizing offer for a love-famished woman.

On a whim she bought herself a ring of interwoven vines, symbolizing growth and unity. "A promise to myself of the good life I was determined to get, *my way*."

The conflicts grew more intense, the jealous suspicions more ugly, driving Elaine deeper into the arms of her knight in shining armor.

Elaine shared openly of her anguish and misery with her best friend Leigh. "I knew what Elaine was doing was wrong," Leigh said, "but I was inexperienced in godly counsel. In my view Elaine was using Scripture to rationalize her desires to end her marriage and run to the man of her dreams." Leigh spent days on her knees consulting God about the situation, waiting for his perfect timing.

Leigh feverishly prayed for her words to get through to Elaine. "Our relationship had always been honest, with God as our foundation. I was scared for my dear friend but knew I had to speak the truth." She urged Elaine to break off her relationship with Dale.

"But how can I stay with a man I don't love?" Elaine wondered out loud. "I can barely tolerate being in the same house with him."

Leigh went out on a limb to answer, "If you follow God's will, he will bless you, and you'll love Brad again."

A bucket of salt tossed on the wound, but the truth penetrated Elaine's heart, and the sobs came in swift succession. "I'm so ashamed."

"I love you, Elaine. Nothing you ever do can change that. God loves you, and he forgives you."

"I felt the Lord reach out and touch me through Leigh," Elaine shared. "She accepted me despite what I'd done, and she would walk through this mess with me. It was the first time I had ever felt complete unconditional love. I didn't deserve her kindness, especially when I ignored her counsel."

Elaine's heart saw God and her circumstances in a new light. She went from believing she deserved better to thanking God that she didn't get what she actually deserved. Willing to do the right thing, to be a "good" Christian, Elaine still harbored the hope that Brad would give up and leave, freeing her from responsibility.

Meanwhile Brad did the unthinkable: he became a Christian. Somewhat like a foxhole conversion when his heart was under siege. "I saw my need and cried out in desperation to the Lord," he said. Leading Brad in the prayer to accept Christ, Elaine mused at the years she had prayed for his salvation; yet, when the time came, she struggled to rejoice in it.

Vowing to be strong, Elaine tried to sever the ties with Dale. Struggling with his own sin, Dale agreed—they had no choice—but in moments of weakness, a phone call for comfort in his loneliness or an "innocent" cup of coffee would set them back into their fantasy romance. Like the old country western song goes: "How can it be so wrong when it feels so right?" She had finally found the "love of her life"; why couldn't she keep him?

Life at home was full of daily arguments, constant tension, and threats of violence. When Brad saw the phone bills, proof of lengthy calls to Dale, he went over the edge. In a frenzy he drove straight to the San Francisco airport, certain some time at his sister's house in Hawaii might help him cool his heels.

Elaine fell to her knees in desperation. How had things gotten so out of control? *How can this be where God wants me, giving up the love I've sought my whole life?* Her mind drifted back to her lonely childhood with a single mother, always dreaming of her knight in shining armor.

Startled to hear the front door open, she glanced up to see Brad toss his suitcase in the hall. "I couldn't get on the plane," he choked.

She was unprepared for her next spoken words. "Please . . . don't leave." Cringing at what had come out of her mouth, she knew it was the Holy Spirit confirming what she must do, give herself to this marriage.

As she told me this, I heard those words waft through my mind again: *Obedience is God's answer to your problem.*

"I sank into depression. I felt trapped, robbed of the love I desperately needed," she said. "I resigned myself to my fate, convinced I would never truly be happy."

One distraught day, Elaine was driving in Dale's neighborhood. "I was so tempted to talk to him, but I sped past his house and pulled in at the park." On the passenger seat was the book Leigh had given her, *After the Locusts,* written by her friend and former workmate—yours truly, Jan Coleman. "For three hours in the park I read stories of how God redeems our pain and turns it to good when we're obedient," she said. "The veil of deception lifted. How could I get trapped into thinking a man who would pursue a married woman was any kind of a catch?"

Elaine went home and locked herself in her office studio. As an artist who relates to symbolism, she fashioned a heart from clay, and when it was dry, she took a hammer to it. "It signified my own heart, battered and broken. I placed the promise ring inside and displayed it on my shelf. I was finally willing to give it all to the Lord."

Slowly Elaine climbed out of her depression, but it took almost a year for the marriage to begin to mend. "We each had to grow individually," Brad said. "And be filled with Christ's love first." Elaine learned to show mercy and grace to her husband. She kept telling herself, "In God's strength, not mine."

For the first time in ten years of marriage, Brad began to open up and share his raw feelings. "I saw behind his walls, his fear of love and intimacy. He was afraid to love and be left." Once he felt secure that she was committed to the relationship, no matter what, the walls tumbled down.

Elaine devoured every marriage self-help book she could find in an attempt to unlock the secrets of her broken past and poor decisions. When she found *Boundaries in Marriage,* she invited Leigh and her husband to join them in a study. With commitment to God as their foundation, Elaine and Brad began to see the unhealthy patterns that had led them to the brink of disaster.

"Every subject that came up, we had faced," Brad said. Couples with shaky marriages witnessed their change and saw a glimmer of hope that their relationships might be salvaged, which springboarded into a second class. "They sought us out for encouragement. If God could heal our marriage, he could heal others that appeared equally as hopeless."

"Two years later God has worked so abundantly in Brad's life; he's so vulnerable and open, a complete opposite of what he was before," Elaine told me over a steaming bowl of wonton soup. "He's on fire for Christ and a warrior for men's accountability groups."

"Men need to risk sharing, to take off their masks," Elaine says and Brad is leading the way.

Now these two spend hours talking about the mysterious workings of God. With a satisfied smile, Elaine said, "I'm so in love with him."

God breathes new life into dry bones.

Just what Ezekiel told the exiled Jews. This faithful prophet had many visions from God. In one the Lord guided him on an inspection tour through a valley strewn with dry bones, a vision of the spiritually dead Jews. "Can these bones live?" the Lord asked.

Ezekiel gave the standard answer, "Lord GOD, [only] You know" (Ezek. 37:3).

The Lord spoke to the bones. "I will cause breath to enter you, and you will live. I will put tendons on you, make flesh grow on you, and cover you with skin. I will put breath in you so that you come to life. Then you will know that I am the LORD" (Ezek. 37: 5–6).

Sometimes a relationship can seem like a pile of dead bones, lifeless and without hope, but God promises to restore marriages, friendships, and family ties that have gone stone cold.

He never stops making the call to come back to him, to let him refresh and renew. If our number comes up busy, he keeps hitting the "redial" until we answer, no matter how long it takes.

My author friend Nancy Anderson made this discovery years ago. "After our wedding Ron and I assumed it was the other person's job to make us happy. We soon found out that was impossible. I complained and criticized my way through our first year. Our anger and resentment grew until it overshadowed our love." Two years later the marriage was dead. "We were both miserable."

That's when Jake came into the picture. "He thought I was beautiful, funny, and smart. He saw only the good in me. We started meeting for workday lunches and dinners. I knew exactly what I was doing. I chose to enjoy his lingering gaze, enjoy his flirtations, and welcome his kiss. I chose to have an affair."

This time God used discerning parents to force self-examination. "I think you're in some sort of trouble," Nancy's mother said. "I woke up last night and felt compelled to pray for you. Talk to your father; he's on the other line."

Gulp. She could never lie to him. He shot straight, "Are you in need of prayer?"

She hesitated. "Yes." And then she delivered the bombshell; she was leaving her marriage. Her dad uttered a prayer that changed everything. He prayed, "that I'd be able to see the destruction I was causing and I'd stop it before it was too late." After she hung up, she made another call, to God. "I had been avoiding him for months. My guilt, shame, and sin had built a wall between us. But as I surrendered my will and my heart, I broke through that wall and asked God for the strength to make a full confession to Ron. Miraculously, he chose to forgive me."

Surrender is the key.

Ron and Nancy rebuilt their marriage with Jesus as their new foundation, "and God's Word as our floor plan. Ron and I are living proof that no marriage is beyond repair."

Being living proof, isn't that what it's all about? The couple recently celebrated their twenty-fifth wedding anniversary, and they conduct couple's retreats and marriage seminars. Nancy has authored a book about affair proofing your marriage, avoiding The Greener Grass Syndrome.

Both women admit that self-centeredness was at the root of their pain. (And as Carl read the final draft of this book, he commented, "That's everyone's problem, Jan.") And they might still be chasing the mirage of fantasy love, repeating their unhealthy patterns, without a transformed heart.

Which comes after you risk the first step of obedience.

Ezekiel gives one of God's greatest promises in the Old Testament when he tells the Jews what will happen when they return to their homeland: they will receive the gift of an undivided heart. "I will give you a new heart and put a new spirit within you; I will remove your heart of stone and give you a heart of flesh. I will place My Spirit within you and cause you to follow My statutes and carefully observe My ordinances" (Ezek. 36:26–27).

While the old covenant was written on stone, the new covenant would be engraved on people's hearts.

A stubborn, rebellious heart works against God's best in our lives. It weakens and deceives us. It's a heart self-obsessed, with crust like two-day-old French bread, and it screams, "Lay off. Let me go my own way."

If we stop running from our pain and discontent, we will hear God's voice saying, "This is what I want you to do," but often we hear the sound of our own voice speaking from a divided heart, rattling off a dozen excuses. *It's too hard. It's unfair. This is not the life I planned.*

The undivided heart allows us to tune in to the Father's voice alone. "Obey Me, and then I will be your God, and you will be My people. You must walk in every way I command you so that it may go well with you" (Jer. 7:23).

There it is—the plum, the prize, the pot at the end of the rainbow, waiting for those who call Jesus "Lord." *So that it may go well with you.* And to take it one step further; *so that it may be used for God's glory.*

When we tackled the adultery/divorce/remarriage issue in our Sunday school class, I shared Elaine and Brad's remarkable story. I choked up repeating Brad's statement, "We are so grateful not to be passing on the curse of divorce."

I set before you a blessing and a curse. What do you choose?

These are prickly squirm-in-the-seat subjects, as our absent class members proved that day. And you or someone you love might be saying: *But you don't know my situation.* So true, and I'm not touting a one-size-fits-all solution. I don't have a miracle marriage turnaround story—and wish I did for so many reasons —but I do know this: No relationship is so dead that God cannot revive it with a joint decision to be willing—a radical idea in today's age of one-click divorces. If you know Jesus, you know what kind of business he's in—the resurrection business.

Only God can stir the embers and breathe new life into old bones, and it's for one mighty purpose: to exalt his holy name.

There is a postscript to Elaine and Brad's story. Leigh phoned me last week with the news that Elaine just discovered she is battling serious cancer. "Jan, you wouldn't believe Leigh about it, how God is using this at ch

Oh, yes I can.

While Elain with saddling Brad with a sick wife, he sees it as his opportunity to show her and the world exactly how much he loves her. His biggest fear can now be put into God's hands. "If the worst happens and we don't beat this,

I'm at peace with Elaine leaving me now because I'll be placing her into the Lord's loving arms, and no other."

Elaine is grateful that the cancer didn't show up two years ago, "before I understood God's character and the width of Brad's love. In my obedience to God, he fashioned the shining armor to fit my husband. I've truly found my storybook hero."

There's a moral strength that comes
from being tested.

holding the party line

chapter 7

What kind of man cheats on his wife? It was a pointed question followed by a woman's voice in reply: "Bill Clinton. Gary Condit. *Dennis Hollingsworth.*"

This ad went out over the airways during a heated race for the California State Senate, and it pulled no punches. It wrapped up with a commentator saying, "You are a hypocrite when it comes to marriage, and you know that."

Guilty as charged—yes—but Dennis Hollingsworth is no hypocrite. Last week I sat across from the senator in his second-floor office at the state capitol, with his chief of staff in the adjoining chocolate leather chair. On the credenza behind his desk was a gallery of family photos, and on display against the dark paneled wall was a framed copy of the U.S. Constitution. Senator Hollingsworth had agreed to take a few moments out of his busy day to talk about standing for God in the combat zone of politics.

My first questions were about his quantum leap into public office. "My dad was a dairy farmer but had his hand in

Republican politics," he answered, "so it was always a subject of discussion around the dinner table." Dennis found his way into a position with a rural county farm bureau. "I'd go up to Sacramento or over to Washington, D.C., regularly to lobby on issues like property rights protection for farmers. I never gave a thought to running for office."

His politically astute, Christ-following friends did it for him. *Won't you consider tossing your hat in the ring for the open assembly seat? The current candidate is a guy vastly opposed to our values.*

First Dennis conferred with his pastor, keeping in mind the ultimate goal of any decision—to seek to glorify God.

"It was six months of persistent prayer and godly counsel. I consulted Christians who knew the ins and outs of politics, as I believe God works and speaks partly through other believers. It seemed a go."

But he was running against three mayors of the largest cities in the district; one had millions to spend. Dennis was largely unknown with a meager campaign war chest. Still, as a strong conservative, he was seen as a formidable threat.

So the enemy camp got ready to drop an A-bomb.

In a confident, composed manner so characteristic of one who has been refined by fire, Dennis said, "A few years prior I had committed adultery." Now Jan, the self-proclaimed ace reporter, had not done her research and knew nothing about this. My friend and long-term confidant chief of staff had not mentioned it either. I clutched my pen in mid note, not out of shock from the surprise admission but from his honesty in calling it by its official name: *adultery.*

Not "affair" or "marital infidelity." No glossing over what it really was, the freewill violation of the marital contract.

"It was the turning point in my spiritual life," the senator continued. "Before that, I was a fire-insurance Christian. It took the full-force realization of the fullness of my sin, the breaking faith with God and my wife, to wake me up." The woman involved filed a workers' compensation stress claim, which was eventually dismissed, but found its way to public knowledge during his run for office.

Dennis is cast in the same mold as King David, a man with stagnant faith who had foolishly drifted into sin but when finally confronted cried out, "Create in me a clean heart, O God" (Ps. 51:10 KJV).

But it was just the kind of juicy pay dirt that opposition research teams love to uncover.

Dennis had only one option—one that seemed right—to come clean and admit it publicly before the smear campaign hit the newspapers. "I had twenty-four hours to prepare. First, we called my pastor and some close friends for prayer, and then we went to visit my family to let them know what to expect from tomorrow's headlines." But his wife's family was unaware it had happened at all. The couple saw no reason to tell them since their marriage had not only survived the crisis but had grown deeper in spite of it, so a tell-all so long after the fact was tough. "But they stood with us."

Just thirty minutes before facing the throng of cameras and microphones, Dennis chanced a call to an old friend in Idaho. "As a congresswoman, she'd been through this, and when she answered the phone, she was actually in a meeting with a group of pastors in her office." He choked up telling me this one. "She put me on the speaker phone, and they prayed with me."

What a way to practice 2 Corinthians 1:4—to comfort others in trouble with the comfort we too have received from Christ.

Finally giving his statement to the public, Dennis felt "God was holding me up. He would take care of it. If I lost the race, I'd lose with my integrity in place."

And the God of sudden upsets worked overtime at the polls. The thirty-two-year-old farmer's son won the race by an eight-point margin.

Then, only nine months into his new job and still learning the ropes, the state senate seat for his district came open, and the local movers and shakers urged him to run. "I sat down with my pastor and the elders of my church. Any decision I made involved them as they were tasked with holding me accountable."

We've sent you off as a missionary to the state capitol, Dennis. If you feel God wants you in the state senate, we're with you.

"I had no money, little name identification, and the district had been redrawn. Plus, I knew the mud would be slung at me all over again. It wasn't going to be easy."

He called that right. But the call on his heart said "go."

The mudslinging—far more vicious than the first go-round— boomeranged, and the voters moved the unapologetic conservative into the upper house. Less than two years after taking the oath to "faithfully discharge the duties upon which I am about to enter," Dennis became a member of one of the most powerful political institutions in the country, the California State Senate.

When I asked him about his greatest challenge, I half expected a soft pound with the fist and an idealistic answer, *fighting for Christian values against the forces of evil.* Without hesitation, he answered, "Time for a faithful prayer life and Bible study."

On his desk sat a book study by John MacArthur. "God is doing a work here at the capitol," he added. "Individual believers are getting stronger, and we're finding our niche ministries. Mine is as a disciple of individual men growing them up in the faith."

Dennis stepped up to serve as chairman of the Proposition 22 Legal Defense Fund. The initiative, passed by a majority of California voters defines marriage as being between a man and a woman, but is being threatened by proponents of same-sex unions.

A moral strength of character comes from passing a test as Dennis did. His future choices will forever be filtered through the lens of what is right in God's eyes.

God loves to use people like that.

It is not what we do that matters but what a sovereign God chooses to do through us. As Senator Hollingsworth well knows, God does not want our success; he wants us, and it often comes at a price. Only the courageous are willing to pay it.

My trek to my old workplace, the state capitol, brought back memories of my years there, specifically the bulletin board above my desk tacked with quotes from the founding fathers. William Penn said, "Unless virtue guides us our choice must be wrong."

During my time there I saw many well-intentioned men and women arrive in Sacramento with an eagerness to make a difference, but some soon joined the ranks of the mugwump, preferring to side with the majority if it would bring them popularity and a plum committee position. Maybe they weren't as sure of their ideals as they thought.

As Dennis explained, "You don't have to agonize over decisions when you are firm in your beliefs, when you know where you stand."

When you're a legislator like Senator Hollingsworth your agenda is not to fight for partisan principles but to work as a disciple for Jesus. Like Patrick Henry's not-so-famous line, "I am no longer a Virginian, Sir, but an American." Once he followed freedom's call, he joined the team, working for a cause bigger than himself.

Wherever we work, our identity is not in what we do, not the title on our business card or what we list as a mailing address. We're no longer Californians or Missourians or New Yorkers. Nor are we what it states on our voter registration either. We're not Republicans, Democrats, or Independents, but Christ followers.

Reflecting the character of the God we serve and promoting his principles with honor.

View tragedy as God's tool to give you
new direction in your life.

from prison to purpose

chapter 8

Pat Nolan was climbing the legislative ladder. He was the Republican leader of the state assembly when I knew him, pitted in daily jousting with Speaker Willie Brown. Those were exciting days to be a state house staffer. Before the 1988 elections, Pat was poised to become the speaker, the second most powerful politician in the state. Next stop, said the Washington pundits, attorney general or maybe even governor.

Instead he got swept up in a federal sting operation. "I was forced to plead guilty and sent to prison for three and a half years," Pat said. Overnight he lost his career, his reputation, and the means to earn a living for his family. So what happens when you're one of the state's fastest rising stars and you're thrown into the pit?

You either become a jerk—bitter and blaming—or a Joseph.

Pat chose Joseph. He trusted God not only to endure the devastating setback in his life but also to see him turn it into triumph. A reminder that it's not what happens to us in life but how we respond to it that builds our character.

Before his release Pat prayed daily about his future and what kind of job to seek. He had a law degree, but politics had been his passion and dream, a door now closed forever. For the last year and a half of his sentence, he would be released to a halfway house in Sacramento. "But I had no idea how I would be employed once I got out. I was getting pretty anxious, and my prayers became more intense."

In the full pitch of a prison it's hard to find quiet time, so Pat's dialogues with God took place while working out on the treadmill or the stationary bike. "I usually put in about forty-five minutes on a machine four or five times a week. During one of these workouts, I talked to God about my job situation. For some reason we weren't connecting. After about twenty minutes I stopped in the middle of my workout and went out to walk the track, where I started in again on my prayers.

"It was a beautiful day; the sky was a gorgeous blue. I stopped, looked up to heaven, and said, 'God, what do I do?'"

The answer came. *I will take care of your family.*

"I can't say that I heard an audible voice, but it was just that real. Not an answer that could have come from me and my insecurities."

He mulled it over. *I will take care of your family. What does that mean?* "It's so nebulous and nondescript, and I'm a 'let's get the facts' kind of guy. I was looking for practical advice, the next step for me to take."

The voice echoed. *"I will take care of your family."*

Like a good lawyer, Pat started summing up the case: *I married late in life. I have to make up for the lost years of income.* "As if he didn't already know the details."

God interjected after every argument: *I will take care of your family.*

Pat finally relented and rested his defense. *God, I have no idea what you have in mind. And I still don't have any idea what I am supposed to do. But you have always blessed me throughout my life; every chapter has been better than the one before. So I thank you in advance for what you will do.*

"He hadn't answered my specific questions, but he had assured me that he would take care of the problem. That's all I needed to know." Then he was called to report to Control A. Being a resident of Dorm B, being called to Control A usually meant some kind of disciplinary action. *Oh, no, what petty little infraction will they jump on me for now?*

Merely a phone call that had come in for him. *That's odd,* he thought, *prisoners don't receive phone calls.* Pat dialed the number—collect of course—and spoke to Jim Schraeder.

"Have you ever heard of Justice Fellowship?" Jim asked him.

"Yes, it's the public policy arm for Chuck Colson's Prison Fellowship. I've seen the literature. I am very impressed with their work."

"They're looking for a president," Schraeder said. "Would you be interested in interviewing for the job?"

It seemed too good to be true—less than an hour and a half after his conversation with God about his future. Prison Fellowship was on the hunt for someone to head up their efforts to reform the criminal justice system, someone familiar with the way government works, used to working with state and federal policymakers, one who could articulate the message of restorative justice.

It had Pat's name written all over it.

"Jim, this has got to be the only job in the country where being in prison is a résumé enhancer. I'm interested." A formal telephone interview was set for a week later. *So is this·how you will take care of my family, Lord?*

Could there be a job more perfectly matched to my interests, skills, and background? Pat wondered. *It would knit together my training as a lawyer, my experience in the legislature, and my time in prison. What an answer to prayer.*

Before the interview, Pat picked up his *God's Word for Each Day* devotional Bible, and the day's verses were from Nehemiah 11–13. God calls his people to go back and rebuild Jerusalem, their capitol, and the ending prayer was this: *Today, ask God to help you be flexible so that you can change jobs or communities when it is according to his plan for you.*

Quite a prayer before an interview for a job that would require a fifth-generation Californian to relocate his family across the country to the outskirts of our national capital.

Justice Fellowship had been searching for the right candidate for eighteen months. None seemed quite right until a not-so-chance encounter between Chuck Colson and Pat. "Word reached us that Chuck Colson was coming to speak at an Angel Tree fund-raiser," Pat told me. "The chaplain often took a group of inmates to church-related events. Once again, the *Deus ex machina*—the hand of God altering events according to his plan and prerogative—came into play. I was eager to be a Prison Fellowship volunteer when I got out and anxious to meet Chuck."

Of the few inmates asked to give their testimony, Pat was one. "I talked about the wonderful impact the Angel Tree visit had on my children. And after his keynote Chuck was whisked off to another appearance."

What Pat didn't know was that on the flight home Colson dictated a memo: *Track down Pat Nolan. He might be the guy we are looking for.*

"I had been fretting about what I would do after prison. Yet it is now obvious that long before I surrendered the whole question, God had this plan in mind. Proverbs 3:5–6 says, 'Trust in the LORD with all your heart and lean not on your own understanding; in all your ways acknowledge him, and he will make your paths straight' (NIV). This was a life-changing lesson in trust."

Back in the midst of the FBI investigation, a good friend had told Pat, "The Bible tells us to trust in the Lord. It doesn't say 'hope.' It says 'trust.'"

Pat had never pondered the difference, but this gave him real insight. "When we hope, we ask God to help us achieve what *we* want," Pat stressed. "When we trust, we ask God to show us what *he wants* us to achieve. When we hope, we rely on *our own* plans. When we trust, we rely on *God's plans.*"

Going to prison was a painful and humbling experience for Pat, but he and his wife Gail came out of it with transformed hearts. "I always knew he was watching out for me, but I thought I had to be the initiator. As a political activist and a legislator, I was a person of faith. I regularly prayed that God would *bless* my efforts. It wasn't until my prison experience that I realized I had it backward. I wasn't supposed to come up with the plan and ask God to bless it. My job was to ask him what his plan was and *then go do it.*"

Alexander Solzhenitsyn said, "I praise you, prison, for what you've done to me."

"Ditto," Pat said. "I went into prison believing in God. I came out knowing him."

The board of Justice Fellowship was meeting a few months later and requested that Pat and Gail fly back for a personal interview. California Board of Prisons regulations allow inmates to travel outside the district for legitimate job interviews. "And what more *legitimate* potential employer than Prison Fellowship?" Pat said. His paperwork was submitted through the proper channels, and Pat waited and waited until the word came down—request denied. *"Does not serve a legitimate interest."*

Huh—now what?

But God's plan cannot be thwarted. The Justice Fellowship board flew five people out to Sacramento to meet with Pat. "Can you imagine that? Not many prospective employers would go to all that effort, particularly when the interviewee is a convicted felon."

When he received the formal job offer, though the salary and benefits were far below what he expected to be earning at this stage in his professional life, Pat would not dare say no. "It was clear that it was God's plan, the plan he'd been preparing me for for a long time. For fifteen years I thought he wanted me in the legislature to make good laws. Now I understand he had been preparing me for *this work*. And my time in prison was necessary because I had to see firsthand the impact of the policies we crafted in the legislature so I could speak credibly about them to lawmakers now."

Pat is a different man from the deal-maker I knew at the capitol. He sported a friendly, confident smile back then, and while his head wasn't overswelled, he was a busy negotiator in strategy huddles with other legislators who valued his opinion and experience. He was a *somebody*, proud of his accomplishments.

In prison his brief claim to fame was worthless. To survive he would need to develop a new frame of mind. Pat pored over Joseph's story—a man sold out by those he trusted but redeemed in an amazing way. When his brothers came to Egypt for help, Joseph revealed himself, and rather than condemning them as they feared, he forgave them.

In the end, those who pursued and sought to destroy Pat were the instruments God used to bring new purpose for his life.

He can mimic what Joseph told his brothers, "Do not be distressed or angry with yourselves for selling me. It was not you who sent me here, but God. You planned evil against me; God planned it for good" (Gen. 50:20).

The eternal perspective of success—
"Walk in a way worthy of me."

true grit

chapter 9

Teresa Tomeo never dreamed God would ask her to walk away from her beloved career as a news anchor. As swiftly as she rose to the top, she fell from favor in a fickle industry and lost her job. "One night I was reporting the lead story on the evening news, and the next minute I was on the unemployment line."

When she was a child, her older sisters dolled up Teresa and gave her the microphone at the annual family Christmas show. From then on she was hooked on performing. Her gift of gab teamed with her talent for writing made a journalism career the sure fit for this feisty brunette.

Growing up in a strong Christian family, she had parents who made prayer and faith a central part of the home. "I first fell in love with Jesus when I was young," she said. "I knew he was real and that he loved me. The problem was, I started having success far too early and was slowly pulled away by worldly desires and goals."

After journalism school Teresa met Dominic, and they became what Teresa calls "Christmas and Easter Christians." After

Teresa made the big jump into television, she rarely saw her engineer husband. Despite their surprising and seemingly endless success, their hearts were empty. "Seven years into our marriage my husband started searching for something more. A mutual friend invited Dominic to a Bible study where he committed his life to Christ," Teresa said. "But I was still in la-la land trying to be a news goddess. If the religious thing worked for him, fine, but I had my own agenda."

As an anchor she was the darling of Detroit. "My reporting assignments took me across the country covering some of the most significant stories of the '90s—the Oklahoma City bombing, a visit by Pope John Paul II, and many others. I was right in the thick of things, loving every minute of it."

Teresa admits to living a "pretty sinful lifestyle," one that took a toll on the marriage, but Dominic never gave up as he watched his wife grow angry at God for losing her job. "Why would he take away my passion, the one thing I could excel at? My lifeblood, the thing I was created to do. I blamed the Lord for all my troubles."

Never realizing what really lay at the core of the problem.

"My entire identity had been in the media. I was *Teresa Tomeo* the television star, not Teresa Tomeo the *Christ follower* and *wife.* Now it was all ripped away. I had no direction, no interest in anything else." During her hiatus from work, in the quiet hours at home, she heard the counsel of God for the first time. "For whoever wants to save his life will lose it, but whoever loses his life because of Me will find it" (Matt. 16:25–26). What will it benefit a man if he gains the whole world yet loses his life?

A puzzling truth ignored in the past, now haunted her daily thoughts.

In *Renovation of the Heart,* Dallas Willard explains those words of Jesus this way: Those who think they are in control—the master of their fate and captain of their soul—find that they definitely are not in control and totally at the mercy of forces beyond them, on the sure course to disintegration and powerlessness. Of *lostness* to themselves and to God.[1]

The only thing left for Teresa to do was surrender.

"What had I become in my quest for success?" she asked herself. "What had I sought to worship?" I took a good look in the mirror, and it was gruesome.

OK Lord, if you're the same Jesus I first met, then please come back into my life and take over, because I have really made a big mess of things.

So she made a trade—her agenda for God's, and what a deal it turned out to be.

Two weeks later an ABC affiliate called and offered her another job. "Wow. God works fast! This time, though, I was committed to seeking his will, not mine. Dominic and I had pledged to make Christ first in our lives. Church, weekly Bible study, and a Christian counselor to help us sort things out took priority."

And she praises God for her husband's faithfulness. "You know, Jan," she told me, "his name, *Dominic Pastore*, translated from Italian to English, means "Shepherd of the Lord." Pretty awesome!"

So she jumped back into the limelight. "And it was like my personal Damascus Road, where the scales started to fall from my eyes. Everything looked different. I now had a clear, commanding view of the profession I had zealously poured my energy into."

The mass media, what Teresa calls "the devil's mouthpiece."

The glamour was gone and with it her penchant for ignoring the dark side of her profession, the one that condones violence and promiscuity and makes a mockery of marriage and family.

But Lord, why did you bring me back here? I thought you'd chosen me to make a difference in secular media.

Yes, but for something far different from what you have imagined. And you had to come back to see the big picture, to get the God's eye view.

"I felt him urging me to use my gifts and experiences to speak out against the problems in our society. So I said good-bye to all of it, walked away from the glitz and prestige and never looked back."

Before long she was hosting a daily talk show on Christian radio in Detroit, using her peppy personality to encourage listeners to put their faith into action. She now conducts awareness seminars to provide the tools to make a difference in the media.

"Not one bit of my time was ever wasted. My background, training, and talents are all being used by God for the greater good. What I am now doing is so far removed from my earlier expectations, but wouldn't you know—God had it in mind all along. He was waiting for me to lay down my plans and consent to his. I had been lost to myself and to him, but now I'm found. And now I'm so fulfilled."

With more wisdom than she ever thought to ask for, the wisdom of Solomon when he wrote, "I have seen all the things that are done under the sun and have found everything to be futile, a pursuit of the wind" (Eccl. 1:14).

I asked Teresa for her favorite verse, and it's Psalm 37:4: "Delight yourself in the LORD and he will give you the desires of your heart" (NIV).

"This verse really sums up my definition of success. Delighting in the Lord should be our focus, our purpose, our reason for living. When the Lord first put the desire on my heart to go into communications, I wanted to use my talents to make a difference. I fell away, deceived by the world's definition of success. Despite all the worldly achievements, I was never truly happy or fulfilled and kept looking for something more. Now I have Jesus back in my life and am delighting in him—that is, putting him first.

"This is to me the real meaning of success. I now have the desires of my heart. But it is all about him not me. I am using my speaking and writing skills, as well as my broadcasting experience, to do my part in preaching the gospel. Funny how this thing works, isn't it?"

As a former pastor friend of hers once said, the Bible is really an acronym:

Basic

Instructions

Before

Leaving

Earth.

King Solomon wrote an enlightening tale of what happens when we strive for success and forget God. Here was a man who built grand palaces, cities, vineyards, and parks but discovered that unless the Lord builds our house, there is no return on the investment. "Better one handful with rest, than two handfuls with effort and pursuit of the wind" (Eccl. 4:6).

Bill Barber is another one who discovered this, and his story has the makings of a great movie.[2] Last year, while flipping through a magazine left in my room at a conference center, an article title, "Sacrificing Success," grabbed my eye. And the content of the piece grabbed my heart.

The author introduced Bill as a kid with "stars in his eyes," a film aficionado who lived for the weekends at the Rialto Theatre in Memphis, daydreaming about what it would be like to work there. His first job was operating the popcorn machine, soon graduating to usher before wearing the assistant manager hat. Fast-forward years later, and the credits are rolling. Bill wrote a blockbuster script for himself as corporate vice president and general manager of United Artist Theaters. He's hobnobbing the country with the stars, arranging for world premier openings.

Money, authority, and influence. He has it all.

But the close-ups reveal the behind-the-scenes action. As he approached a generous retirement, Bill's wife Nanette had been growing in her faith (The Lord works this way so many times, doesn't he?) and praying for her husband to have a real encounter with the Lord.

And the persistent God went to work. "I discovered that he desired to take over every area of my life, including my job," Bill says. Matthew 18:6 flashed like a neon sign: "But if anyone causes one of these little ones who believe in me to sin, it would be better for him to have a large millstone hung around his neck and to be drowned in the depths of the sea" (NIV).

That's you, Bill.

"It was as if I had been stabbed in my heart, and I cried out in repentance for my part in promoting films that had been so against God's principles."

He had only one choice and announced it the next day; he would leave his position in the company. Though urged to reconsider, Bill stood firm. As the article's author, Greg Asimakoupoulous, notes, this might not be a *must do* for everyone facing a similar situation, but it was the right move for Bill. For him to honor God's claim on his life.

"I know without a doubt, I did the right thing. The Lord has confirmed it time and again in the way he's provided for my family and me. I needed to lose everything I had taken pride in so that I could discover his ability to take care of me."

Finally, after two years of unsuccessful job searching, Bill found employment—with a church janitorial service. From up-close and personal with the stars—to cleaning toilets?

Bill had come a long way.

His lifelong interest in entertainment has led him on different roads—to serve as a consultant for Billy Graham's worldwide pictures, for one—and he's since been using his professional experience for God.

Prior to meeting Jesus, the apostle Paul—Saul of Tarsus who persecuted those preaching the gospel—held the privilege of dual citizenship, Roman and Jewish. Most people in the empire were not Roman citizens, so it was a special status. A member of the Sanhedrin, the Jewish high court, he was a man of standing in the community.

On the way to Damascus, he had a vision of blinding light and heard the voice of Jesus, and for three sightless days he struggled with his newly aroused conscience. He had been chosen to walk away from his former life and travel the world for Christ, and he never looked back.

"I was not disobedient to the heavenly vision" (Acts 26:19), Paul told King Agrippa.

Obedience often means walking away from a comfortable lifestyle, letting go of a former identity, but when we nod to the vision and turn our steps toward it, the benefits are a stronger character, a deeper commitment, and an enhanced love for the one who leads the way.

He doesn't take us out of the world but
wants to use us in it.

of the world
but not in it

chapter 10

At the age of twenty-six, in 2000, Brandon Slay won the Olympic gold medal in freestyle wrestling in Sydney, Australia. The ultimate achievement, right? Not for Brandon; his mission is now to urge athletes to seek the "Greater Gold."[1]

Proverbs 16:16 says, "How much better to get wisdom than gold, to choose understanding rather than silver" (NIV).

When you enter Brandon's Web site, you are greeted with: "This site began as young people started asking for my autograph. Soon after, I realized my name will never do anything for anybody. However, I hoped my thoughts and heartfelt feelings on life could do something for somebody. They say evil triumphs when good men do nothing. This is one of the ways in which I'm attempting to do something. If you are curious about the passion that pours from my soul like a running river, please click the *Greater Gold* link above and go to the *Belief System* link . . . You will learn more about our mission and how we use sports to plant positive seeds of hope in the lives of our nation's youth."

For many years he tried to accomplish his wrestling dreams without God; then he realized his life was empty and only God could bless the desires of his heart. At the end of 1999, he gave his life completely up to Christ. With new spiritual strength he was able to go from sixth in the nation to first in the world.

He had to lose his life to find it.

"If we are obedient and doing the natural, God will do the super if it's according to his will," Brandon states.

He offers wrestling camps and clubs to encourage youngsters to reach their full academic and athletic potential. He's a sought-after speaker who travels the country speaking to schools, youth groups, churches, and companies. I first read about him on the Fellowship of Christian Athletes' (FCA) Web site.[2] The story highlighted his speech to a group of women athletes from Texas Women's University. "I used to get drunk all the time, curse daily, and live in sin with my girlfriend," he told the women. "I had to get rid of that junk and begin walking with the Lord daily. How did I do that? I made a commitment to avoid drunkenness. I made a commitment to clean up my foul mouth. I made a commitment to purity."

Two of his listeners turned a corner in their pursuit of Christ through Brandon's challenge, and immediately made a decision to abandon the same sin in their lives.

Brandon likes to tell his audiences, "If you make things and people in life your heaven, they can become your hell." There is nothing more powerful than a personal testimony.

Coach Steve Shipley from Nashville has one, too. He had just finished the best coaching season of his career. "I was one of the winningest high school coaches in the state for my age," he said. "I had a TV show, radio broadcasts. I had really had it made," he wrote in an article for FCA, subtitled, "How one man stopped worshipping the scoreboard."

One summer Coach Shipley attended a camp for the Fellowship of Christian Athletes and heard a speaker ask, "Are you living as God would have you live?" Steve nodded inwardly. *Sure.* Why not? He was a good person, a good father and husband, and active in his church. "To the extent I could see, I had a viable relationship with God."

And then the speaker hit him with his best shot. "Do you worship God or the scoreboard?"

"That was a bit convicting, and I found myself asking the Lord, *Make me the coach, husband, and father you'd have me to be.*"

A sincere and worthy request, simple and refreshing.

How often do we pray, *Lord, make me . . . ?* But how seldom do we understand the process and count the cost? Do we envision the potter at the wheel, remolding and reshaping the clay— our identity—to correct the flaws and defects? Working out the kinks and imperfections, pressing on tender places, pushing and pushing.

This is not a passive prayer for the fast fix.

Coach Shipley never knew how much change would be required of him with that prayer. "From that moment on, my life as I knew it then was over. God began chipping away at the areas that prevented me from being the type of person he would have me to be."

Talk about being cut down to size. The next year his team took a dive, from a thirty-five-win season to a losing record. So the coach switched jobs, twice. "I moved my family and went where I thought God wanted me to be, and despite bringing another team to a championship," it all fell apart. "I was let go and out of a job. It was painful and dehumanizing."

Being an out-of-work has-been coach brought Steve to his knees, he told me recently. "Schools I could have called five years earlier were turning me down. I had lost my name recognition by moving out of the area. Plus, I was no longer a 'golden boy.' I had to learn humility and grace, to be brought to a point where I really acknowledged my need for God."

But the process is not over. "I still fight the desire to have what I once had in the eyes of the world, but daily I am reminded that the real glory is in a growing relationship with a God who loves me."

Ten years have passed, and the coach is a different man both professionally and as a person. "I finally put my relationship with God above coaching and winning. No longer am I defined as a coach who happens to be a Christian but as a Christian who is a coach.

As George "Blood and Guts" Patton said, success is how high you bounce when you hit bottom.

James Sang Lee made a heavenly leap after hitting his bottom. Wisconsin born, he spent his youth active in sports, but when leg injuries sidelined his track-and-field career, he turned to karate. So taken was he with martial arts, he scrapped his school plans to pursue it as a profession and became the national champion in 1991.

Two years later Hollywood producers discovered him, and he proved the perfect stuntman for numerous movies such as *Blade* and *Lethal Weapon 4*.

"I had money, fancy cars, and homes on both coasts. I was greedy for possessions, but I was not happy and definitely not satisfied," he responded in an e-mail interview. "I was doing drugs, drinking heavily, involved with numerous women, and looking for satisfaction in anything I could get my hands on. I competed for titles in martial arts and pursued the movies for adulation, fame, self-worth, and praise. I essentially gained the whole world but was losing my soul."

One night after the premiere of his self-defense video workout, the emptiness finally got to him. "I went home, and all I could do was cry. I got down on my knees and prayed to God to change my life because I was so far from him."[3]

Although he was in his best physical shape—never once injuring himself on the set—a week later James blew out his shoulder socket. Not during one of his death-defying stunts but *while styling his hair.* "It was very painful. While my shoulder healed, my life turned quiet; no fanfare, no red carpet, no people screaming my name, no job, no friends, just time to *think.* I couldn't drive my sports car because I couldn't shift the gears. I just spent time meditating on God's truth. And confronting the habits and addictions that were prohibiting me from knowing and seeing God clearly."

Show me what you want me to see.

The Lord directed him to 1 Corinthians. "Everyone who competes exercises self-control in everything. However, they do it to receive a perishable crown, but we do it for an imperishable one. Therefore I do not run like one who runs aimlessly, or box like one who beats the air. Instead, I discipline my body and bring it under strict control" (1 Cor. 9:25–27).

He looked at the world in a whole new light. "With the restyling of my hair that day, came a restyled life. I had been given something very special—my talent and opportunities—but they weren't just for me; they were also for others. I was blessed so that I should bless others.

"The more I read, the more I saw that God's ways are higher than ours, that heaven is our destination. I sought the things of the world, and they are substitutes. Jesus Christ is the only thing that satisfies."

As God touched his life intimately, he began to question everything he had believed in. "I was reminded that the things I thought were needs were actually just wants. Satisfaction could only come from Jesus Christ.

"From the painful experience of my shoulder blowing out, God redirected my life on a path away from these sinful ways and onto a path close to him. I found Jesus, and I did not need these worldly things anymore. I met Christ. Sold my house, car, gave up the career, status, my thinking, and my life."

He didn't just say, "Yes, I believe in God," but "I know God and belong to him."

There is a difference.

One is merely identity, the other identity with a single-minded purpose. God impressed upon him to "love my people, share the truth with the youth and make disciples of all nations."

So that's what he's doing.

He began boldly sharing the true source of our self-defense.

He's been able to lead many people to Jesus through his martial arts skills. "Some people will come to a karate demonstration who will never come to a church service." James now serves on staff of a sixty-five-hundred-member nondenominational church in Orlando.

Jesus, before he completed his mission on earth, prayed for his disciples and all who followed him. "I am not praying that You take them out of the world but that You protect them from the evil one" (John 17:15).

Don't take them out of the world, but use them in the world.

Strong choices come from strong convictions. Brandon, James, and Coach Shipley are aware of what God has done for them, and this awareness drives what they say and do.

When we stand firm while the world mocks, we
are a witness of the astounding power of God.

bats or bonkers: God's wisdom foolish in the world

chapter 11

Y ou're playing the fool." "You've tried to make it work." "Just
bail out and be done with him," many of her friends urged.

If only she could. After all, Connie had ample reason to give
up on Stormy; their problems surfaced the moment she uttered,
"I do." His excessive drinking, partying with the boys, the angry
outbursts, and worst of all, his resistance to church. Ten years of
an unstable situation and numerous separations. It was more
like a soap opera than the love story Connie had prayed for and
envisioned.

"Booze, the boob tube, and his buddies—those were his priorities," Connie told me during our coffee time at La Bou. "I continually dished up excuses for him."

One thing she wouldn't dish up, though—his walking
papers. Not out of loyalty for the man she married but for her

commitment to God. "My flesh continually wanted to leave, but the Lord kept encouraging me in so many ways, through so many signs, to be steadfast and keep praying. Finally, I prayed that God never let my love for this man die. If it does, the marriage is over."

So what? scoffed the skeptics. *Come on, this is so dysfunctional.* Maybe so, but she could not erase the words Stormy uttered after the ceremony: "Please don't ever leave me," the cries of a little boy desperately wanting to belong. And she couldn't discount what she had vowed, "I promise to love you." "Every person who ever said they loved Stormy, left him," she told me.

There is no need for the tabloid details; it's not critical to the message, but when Connie tumbled into this marriage, she admits that "I wasn't thinking beyond the moment." She already had two young daughters from "other" relationships. She gave me the rolling eyes look. "That says it all right there. We live in a society that blames behavior on our home environment, but I was raised in a good Christian home. I chose to act outside those principles. Suddenly, I was thirty-two, ready to grow up and settle down. And here was someone who finally wanted to marry me."

Right motives, wrong man, right? That's what the world might say.

In the ensuing years God used the almost ceaseless pain to chip away at Connie, to bring her back to her Christian roots. "It was a test. How much can you take in the name of committed love, Connie?"

One evening after Bible study, in a private moment with a friend, Connie mumbled, "Of all the good things I asked for, just look at all the bad things I got."

The friend had a profound comeback. "Connie, how do you know he is not the man you asked for? God only needs to fashion him into it; however, it might take ten years. Are you willing to wait?"

She cried the rest of the night, grappling with her doubts about God and the immense task ahead, bound to a situation that seemed impossible. The Lord seemed to say: "Connie, you believe that I can. Where you struggle is believing that *I will.*"

So true, and it only added to her confusion. *How do you know it isn't going to take this difficult marriage to Stormy to change you? Now that's a twist,* she thought, pondering her friend's words. Her focus had centered on changing Stormy and the situation and struggling with anger at being the condemned woman.

Connie leaned on her handful of trusted confidantes, friends who put aside their own common sense opinions to seek God's viewpoint. Those who understood the message of 1 Corinthians 1:20, "Hasn't God made the world's wisdom foolish?"

Over and over she felt encouraged by these friends to be devoted to Stormy through Christ. "It was impossible to do it alone. God showed me he was with me; a card, a phone call from a friend at the precise moment of need, a Scripture encompassing my exact thoughts and fears. He embraced me, comforted me. It grew less important to get it from Stormy." She asked God to instill her with his nature: "Empty me of me and fill me with you."

When I began planning for this book, Connie's name popped up as I wrote the outline. She attended our church, and I'd been a distant eyewitness to this soap opera for seven years. Bits and pieces of her story kept floating their way into my memory bank.

Stormy's home. Stormy's gone again. The volcano finally erupted. Stormy's in jail for domestic violence. She's finally drawn the line and won't let him come back home.

One morning in a hurried hug in the foyer, she said, "I'm not pursuing a divorce." Though she'd gotten the official go-ahead from pastors and counselors to be released from the marriage if she chose, she didn't. "But things have to change. I've finally given up trying to fix it. The Lord told me, 'Connie, keep praying but *get out of the way.'* I told the Lord, 'If we get back together, *you* will have to bring about some miracle to do it.'"

How about a devastating truck accident with Stormy in critical condition, his body crushed, bones wired and bolted together, a paralyzed face and a gouged eye, its vision lost forever? Plus the terrifying knowledge that he might be responsible for the death involved.

It couldn't get much worse.

As Connie sped up the mountain highway to Reno to be at his hospital bedside after the accident, she felt the spirit of the Lord. *I want you to love and forgive this man, as I love and forgive you.* Reunited with her husband, she saw a stir in his heart, a change in his manner. Something more than an accident had affected him.

"When I woke up in that hospital room, I knew Connie was there," Stormy told me later. "And I was alive. God had spared me. I should have been the one to die, yet another man had died. That's a heavy burden."

When his mangled body could finally walk, Connie helped him get to the second-floor chapel and observed his personal moment with God. "That's when I knew the Holy Spirit was at work," she said. "Finally, I began to see that my obedience in loving him paved the way for this miracle."

For two years Connie nursed her husband back to health and remained quietly supportive as they waited for the outcome of the court trial for involuntary manslaughter. "Though we didn't talk about spiritual things, it was the sweetest time we've ever had."

And they would need those memories to sustain them through his two-and-a-half years of a prison sentence. "When I dropped him off there, I felt so scared and alone. I kept going back to God's promises. Somehow I knew he was going to use this time to turn my husband into the man of my dreams. I went from sorrow to praising the Lord."

Enter the skeptics, at it again. "I could *never* do what you did. What if it's not real?"

But Connie ignored them, refusing to give credence to any talk that would tempt her to fear. Meanwhile, Stormy—and no it is not a nickname; his mother went into labor on a *stormy* night—spent his first twenty-one days in lockup with no contact with anybody except a prison guard. No books, no magazines. "I just lay there night after night weeping, telling the Lord I was sorry for everything I had done, and he let me know it was OK. He loved me, and he was rejoicing that my heart had found its home."

In the first few months he read through the entire Bible twice. Then Connie began the crusade to supply him with his wish list: Christian books. A good friend offered to purchase the books and arranged with a retail store to ship them directly to the prison. "I must have read seven to eight books a week. I devoured every word," Stormy said. "And I always had hated to read."

One evening, "fifteen minutes before chow," a truck pulled up in the yard filled with gift bag "care packages" of soap, shampoo, and personal items, with a book tucked in each one. Most of the inmates ignored the books, so Stormy rounded them up. "They actually opened a library because of all my books."

An accidental ministry, the best kind.

When I met Connie for our impromptu interview, she was on the countdown for Stormy's release, three weeks away. As she sipped on her iced mocha, she told me, "I can't wait to see the fruit of God's labor in his life."

She was excited and scared like a prospective bride. "It's a new beginning for us." She patted her stomach. "I'm a few pounds overweight. Will he care? What will I wear? What will it be like? Especially that first night?"

Then last Sunday during worship, I glanced over and saw Connie waving at me and beaming as she pointed to Stormy. "I'll see you after the service," I mouthed to them.

Pastor Dave was on the third week of a new series in Philippians, "A Garden in My Prison," seeing God's hand in difficult circumstances. He painted a word picture of Paul under house arrest in Rome, chained to a Praetorian guard, knowing his future could likely involve a short walk to the Roman Coliseum to be lion bait. "He has problems, *prozac-level problems*," pastor said. "He has every reason to be stressed out and can relate to the country tune, 'If it weren't for bad luck, I'd have no luck at all.'"

But Paul says this: "What has happened to me has actually resulted in advancement of the gospel" (Phil. 1:12). Don't feel sorry for me, Paul stressed, and see beyond the outward appearances, Pastor Dave urged. View your prison—whatever circumstances you're in—as a way to grow your faith and show what you believe.

To the casual observer Paul appeared to be a victim, the pastor continued. Hey, I know it might look like that, but I'm not the victim, I'm the victor, Paul stressed over and over.

I lost it right there and scoured my purse for a scrap of Kleenex.

The word *advance*, the pastor explained, is a military term, not for merely moving ahead but doing so against obstacles, against resistance. I thought of Connie and her steadfast faith and those who said she was bonkers. Connie in the third row with her husband beside her. Stormy had been at church countless times before, physically present, but never with his whole heart, mind, and soul engaged.

The sermon was about perspective, seeing things God's way. I thought of Hosea, the prophet with a love so strong that even the worst actions of an adulterous spouse could not kill it. While Gomer wandered from home in sin and destruction, Hosea held true to his wife and obedient to his God who said, "Go, show your love to your wife again" (Hos. 3:1 NIV).

It's a beautiful glimpse into God's redeeming heart and

persistent love. Hosea's radical actions represent love despite unworthiness. Connie is my modern-day Hosea.

"I used to go to church for Connie," Stormy told me. "Now I need to go for me."

The three of us met for coffee so I could get some good quotes from Stormy before they moved to Oregon to start a new life. "I look back and see that nothing I've gone through has been a coincidence," he said.

Especially meeting Connie. "She hung in there with me when nobody else would have."

Connie simply took God at his word, hard as it was at times. "Hope does not disappoint," she said. "It may take a while, and for us it took more than ten years. I remember reading a *Daily Bread* once, and these words describe me: *I got nothing I asked for but everything I hoped for.*"

Connie's advice to all of us: "Don't be in such a hurry to run your own life. You'll miss the blessing."

If she had listened to the skeptics instead of God, where would Stormy be? Connie stood firm when it looked like the crazy thing to do.

I can hear the questions that might pop up: Does God really expect us to stand strong in this kind of difficult situation? Stay faithful, put our life on hold? Not always, but if he did and you knew it was his wish for you, how would you respond? I want to think I'd pass the test of faithfulness to God's orders no matter what because I've learned to trust that all things work together for good.

But Connie was chosen for the difficult and extraordinary, to take up her cross and follow Christ in a way that looks foolish to the human eye. She accepted early on that there would be pain involved, but her love for the Lord and her commitment to their covenant relationship superceded her fear and doubts. "Though he slay me, yet will I trust in him" (Job 13:15 KJV).

Through Connie's obedience, God—in his own way and in his own time—defined love to Stormy, and this love proved to be the magnet that drew a rebel to his life-giving Savior.

Stormy has a patch where his eye used to be, and he shuffles along with a limp. Connie describes him as "disabled in body but enabled in spirit."

Only an incredible God can do that through the love of a steadfast heart.

*God never forgets the faithful. His timing is
perfect, and his rewards are never late.*

true blue

chapter 12

Back in my state capitol days, I returned to work from vacation to a pyramid of reports and "to dos" and a perky new staff member at the front desk. Cathy, hired in my absence, proved to be all that her résumé promised and then some. No stranger to the capitol workforce, she'd been on a two-year hiatus after her honeymoon.

And that's the story, one eagerly shared with her new single friend/office manager at every coffee break. "Don't ever compromise, Jan. Wait for the love story only God can write."

I had already decided to do just that.

Cathy's journey to faith was a rocky one. After years enduring an abusive marriage, she ended it. Barely thirty with a young daughter to support, she found employment with a local attorney. "Jack was the wisest and most gentle man I had ever met," Cathy told me during one of the rare moments when the capitol phones weren't ringing. "I was amazed at the peace and calmness in the law firm, even during hectic times."

Jack and his associate held weekly Bible studies before work. "I honestly started going only because it might make a good impression and help me get promoted. Ha! I got promoted all right. I ended up with a free ticket to heaven."

Jack never pressured Cathy about church or asked where she stood with God—not a word—but one day he presented her with a Bible with her name engraved on the cover. "He gently encouraged me to read the book of John."

The rest is history, Cathy says.

"After I became a Christian, nobody urged me to go back to my husband in forgiveness and suggest we try again, but I knew it was the right thing to do, that restoration would please God. My husband refused, wanting nothing more to do with me, eventually fading out of the family scene—as a father too. But I'd given it my best shot."

With her legal experience, Cathy landed a job as a legislative aide at the state capitol. Growing in her faith, she first resisted the temptation for affection from a man, but the lonely and insecure moments were overwhelming. "I had such low self-esteem," Cathy admitted. "I wanted to be desired, so I started 'practice dating,' using all my charms to see if I could just get a guy interested, and it worked! Unfortunately, the only ones that attracted me were non-Christians. *If I could only get him to church*, I'd think, *then he'd change. He would meet the Lord, and we would live happily ever after.*"

A dream that died a hard painful death, a few times too many.

After years of dating the noncommitted, and the half committed, and "getting my heart stomped on a time or two," Cathy finally gave up and gave it over. "I got down on my knees and cried out, *Lord, I can't pick men. Give me the power to have a godly relationship and abstain from sex until marriage.*

"Deep down I knew that God had someone special for me, and then Satan would do his dirty work and send doubts my way. I practiced brushing them off. I realized how many times I'd blown it and how many miracles God performed in my life and those around me. I decided to commit to God's best and nothing less. What freedom to take it out of my hands. God knows me best and will make me the best I can be."

Then harder times came; her mother became paralyzed from a stroke. "The self-pity moments rushed in. I'd clean my mom's apartment, bathe her, do laundry, rush to my daughter's game at school, taxi her everywhere, then drive an hour to see my severely ill grandmother. I cried my little heart out because I was so tired of taking care of everyone else but me."

But at night, when she could have escaped into a good cinema fantasy on television, she'd grab her walkman tape player, pop in a Christian tape, and jog three or four miles through her neighborhood. "Those were the times I'd feel the Lord hold me and assure me—*trust me*—better times were on the way."

Meanwhile her capitol pals kept up the pressure to date. "Because they didn't understand what 'standing for the Lord' means, they'd eye me funny when I'd decline one of their hot prospects. They'd roll their eyes when I'd reaffirm that I was only interested in a committed *Christian* man."

Pretty tall order. Might as well resign yourself to sleeping single in a double bed. "That's right, and it's OK, I'd say. I was completely content waiting on God."

It was far better than the relationship hopping she observed among her friends. "It was so empty, and it never turned out happily ever after. It just made me more determined. The state capitol may be a breeding ground for darkness—the devil is working overtime—but there is light, hundreds of sincere Christians tucked into offices on every floor."

Every Wednesday at noon, Cathy trotted down to the weekly Bible study in an empty committee room. "I was *never* far away from encouragement to keep the faith."

When Cathy noticed a precious friend compromising her values, she asked the group for prayer support and then took time for a sister-to-sister talk. "She was so mad at me for speaking the truth, for urging her to see it from God's point of view. She cut off our friendship."

The cost of standing for God was high, but it never deterred Cathy. "I grew so much during that time of waiting."

How we cope with delays is another test of our loyalty to Christ.

After nine years of going solo, she met Jeff. She chuckled as she related the story. "I never even noticed him as a potential date. I had volunteered to help on a state assembly campaign, and there we were stuffing envelopes and licking stamps together, talking about God and life. And I thought, *Now here is a man who understands what it means to take up your cross and follow Jesus.*" But he was ten years younger than me and had never been married. She wondered, *Now he's quite a catch. Who can I match him up with?*

"Several months later, as he was dropping me off from a campaign workers meeting, he gave me a hug—like the dozens of other hugs we've had—but this time my body zinged all over. It surprised me. I could hardly say good-bye as I shut the door. I went to bed shaking, asking God to clarify this for me. The next morning I knew Jeff was the one for me. A man sold out to the Lord, still single because he was waiting for God's very best."

And their relationship is just that. I've been a witness for the last twelve years as Cathy and I became soul sisters. When asked what Scripture promise she hung on to during those difficult years, Cathy quoted Psalm 37:4: "Delight yourself in the LORD and he will give you the desires of your heart" (NIV).

What is delighting to Cathy? Relishing in God, letting him stir the emotions for his holy purpose, allowing him to possess every thought and attitude. Charles Spurgeon said that if you desire Christ for a perpetual guest, give him all the keys of your heart. Not just one or two cabinets but every room and chamber.

That's what Cathy did. Her arrival in our office was no accident; she had *holy orders*. Her exuberance encouraged and motivated me toward my best. Our histories were so similar—a difficult marriage, a trek on the "looking for love in all the wrong places" highway until finally relinquishing control to the Lord, and more than a decade of being single again.

Cathy was on hand to prep me for my first real date with Carl, a birthday lunch across the street at the Hyatt Hotel, and she bubbled with excitement. After brushing my cheeks with blush and applying her pearly peach lipstick for the final touch, she dished out enough advice to fill an Ann Landers column. After the date—an hour and a half later—she grilled me with questions. Ignoring my schoolgirl giddies, she urged me, "Don't get fooled by your feelings, now. Don't rush it. God is never late."

For sure. I had already had that lesson from Bruce.

He was one of the greenhorn leaders God recruited for an interfaith singles ministry in our small town. Bruce could never figure out why he was chosen for the job; he is not the onstage type of guy—preferring the background—nor is he much of an idea man; and aside from a little guitar strumming, he couldn't claim any noteworthy gifts.

Except his integrity. And—oh—how God used that.

When the four of us—Russ, Jeanne, Bruce, and I—accepted God's challenge to begin the ministry, I looked ahead to tapping into my creativity to offer fun Christ-centered events every week. Bruce looked deeper. "You know, leadership is serious business. We'll be up-front, on display constantly. We'll have to live up to a higher standard."

And he was commissioned to lead the way. Bruce was into his fifth year as a single. His Christian wife of thirteen years had left him for another man, and though he signed the divorce papers, he never stopped praying for reconciliation. During the early days of our ministry, he announced, "As long as she's without a wedding ring on her finger, I'm not dating because I'm not free to remarry."

Wow. Talk about unwavering. Bruce had searched the Scriptures and despite being told that "an unrepentant spouse can be dealt with as an unbeliever" (see 1 Cor. 7:15), Bruce held firm. By this time all his husbandly feelings were dead, but feelings had no bearing on the facts. "In my heart I was not released."

It was not simply the Scriptures; Bruce had made an irrevocable commitment, a covenant, with God as a witness. "When we walk away from God, he doesn't back out of his end of the deal. He waits. If I start dating and open my heart to someone else, I might get in God's way. I won't do that."

How does a man become so steadfast? I wondered, never having met one, at least an unmarried one. In college Bruce accepted Christ knowing what it would cost him, a painful break with the Mormon faith of his Utah family and the disapproval of his parents. Their relationship was never quite the same.

When faith is costly, we value it more.

Bruce never came out and suggested that we follow suit and opt not to date; after all, we'd be meeting many more prospects over the next months, and the opportunity could present itself often. He never openly asked us to dedicate this "season" of life to the ministry. Yet we four leaders, pledged just that, agreeing it was the right thing, to lead by Paul's example: "We put no stumbling block in anyone's path, so that our ministry will not be discredited" (2 Cor. 6:3 NIV).

We determined the group would not be about finding a mate but finding purpose as a single. We had been commissioned to guide a group of wanderers—and some singles saw themselves as misfits and outcasts—who would look to us for inspiration, and our actions would influence them more than we would know. If we went in for smorgasbord dating, so would they.

With this in mind, we focused on building pure and healthy relationships with one another and with God. Bruce began a journey into himself, pausing to ask the questions: "Where did I fail in my marriage? How can I become the best man I can be, whether I'm single the rest of my life or not?"

I'm not one to jump on bandwagons, but this one was headed to heavenly places. *Be the best I can be.* Not one of our planning meetings concluded where one of us wouldn't say in surprise, "We are the ones being blessed by this ministry."

One important discovery for me was that you do not have to be married to be effective for Christ. We four were just where God wanted us to be, enjoying the fruit of Paul's commandment: "Each one should retain the place in life that the Lord assigned to him, and to which God has called him" (1 Cor. 7:17 NIV).

For such a season as this.

Bruce never put it into these words, but his actions spoke them loudly to me: "God calls me to enhance his reputation in my life." *Just where I am.*

It meant resisting the pressure to compromise his beliefs. Like Cathy, he was criticized for his stand. "You're the innocent party, Bruce. Life is short. You're over forty now. If you want a family, better find a nice woman and get to it."

Bruce had become so close to God, so confident in him that no other voices could dull the Father's. Like Paul, in everything Bruce did he considered how his decisions would affect the cause of Christ. He was a man of few words, but his life mirrored every wise one of them.

What woman wouldn't be enamored with a man like that? Suddenly, I had a crush on Bruce and confessed to Jeanne, "This is crazy. Maybe I'd better quit the ministry."

"Don't you dare, let it pass. You've discovered what kind of man you want, one with high principles; and now you'll never settle for anything less." She paused and revealed her little secret.

"The same thing happened to me long ago. It will pass." And it did.

Three years flew by, and when we arrived one evening at Bruce's house for our weekly strategy meeting, he met us at the door in his typical deadpan fashion but with a new greeting. "I just found out my former wife has remarried." His face had an odd look, relief and resignation rolled into one. Seven years of standing firm, accepting the death of his dream, and everything had now changed. "I fought the fight. I have no regrets. I did everything I could, and now—"

He could be open for a relationship, the true desire of his heart.

Bruce kept waiting. There were no potentials in our group, no women remotely near his age who hadn't yet had children but wanted them. Then a friend introduced him to Gwen, a teacher like himself. "She was cute and obviously interested—and so was I—but very wary," he said. And rightly so. After many long talks, he discovered that while Gwen was raised in a traditional church, she did not have a personal relationship with Jesus Christ.

What does one do with a strong attraction to someone who shares your interests and values in every way except the most vital one? The issue of "missionary dating" kept surfacing as a topic in our group, and we were adamant about the wisdom of Paul when he urged believers not to be "mismatched with unbelievers." We'd seen others compromise, tempt fate, and roll the dice, hoping for a quick conversation with their beloved who expressed interest in knowing more about God—until after the wedding. In almost every case the believer looked back in regret and lived spiritually single.

Not a God-designed situation.

That weekend our singles group went to a Victorian Christmas celebration in Grass Valley. As the cars emptied in the parking lot, Bruce and I lagged behind. Sensing his heavy heart, I asked, "You're not OK, are you?"

His deep sigh said it all, another death of a vision. "I really care for her, Jan. She's so perfect in so many ways. But I asked myself, *Am I willing to compromise everything I believe in? Isn't that what my role in this singles ministry is all about?* We teach that there is no middle road with God. I have to be an example of what we teach, standing for God no matter what."

He had no other choice. "I tried to break it to her gently. I told Gwen I couldn't see her again because it couldn't go anywhere."

He told her in a note, no less, because he couldn't face her in person. "It was just so hard."

There was a return note from Gwen the following week. "Exactly what *is* a relationship with the Lord?" she wrote. "I pray. I go to church. Anybody can say they accept the Lord. I don't understand."

And she was very eager to find out.

"I had never met a man like Bruce," Gwen said last week as I met with them in their family room. "There was no chemistry, but he was something unique. In this infamous note—which I still have—were the four spiritual laws, and at first I was miffed at him for sending it, but then I read them over carefully. It was all new to me. I had never heard about confessing your sins before the Lord and accepting Christ, not in my church. I had no idea what saying those words with a sincere heart would mean."

Once she confessed Christ, she crossed her own Rubicon.

But was it sincere, or did she accept Christ just to snag Bruce? My skeptical antennae went up. Finally, Jeanne stepped in. "Let me disciple her and see if she wants the Lord as much as she wants Bruce."

And she did. Gwen started showing up on Saturday nights and joining in like one of the dateless regulars. "Bruce told me we had to start over in a new friendship."

"I wanted to make sure it was God bringing us together," he said. "I had to make sure."

What a testimony to doing it the right way. A year after they met, Bruce and Gwen were married in her parents' yard. She was pregnant six weeks later. "Neither of us knew why we hadn't become parents in our previous marriages," Gwen said, "and being over forty it was questionable it would happen at all. Boy, were we surprised!"

"God is never late," Bruce states with confidence. "Look at us; we're Abraham and Sarah."

Do you recall how the biblical couple harbored doubts about God's promise to bless them with children at their advanced age? Since it was common in those days for an infertile couple to have a family through a surrogate, they took matters into their own hands with a maidservant. They flunked the willingness test, refusing to wait on God to work out his impossible-to-the-human-mind promises in his own way.

On the faithfulness exam Bruce rated an A-plus.

And I took notes. My embarrassing crush—yes, he sensed it and thankfully was kind enough to ignore it and let it run its course—was short-lived. Looking back, it's evident how God positioned me as a friend and eyewitness to this unfolding story. Because Bruce was a man after God's own heart, I set my own remarriage standards heaven high: I would settle for nothing less than a man with whom I could serve God more effectively married than single.

And I would never again be fooled by an imitation.

When Carl came along, it did not take me long to size him up against my living example. I had found my Bruce.

God uses marriage and singleness to accomplish his purposes. If you look on each as God's best for the season, it isn't a burden to wait in obedience for the ideal mate, whether God needs to bring one or build one.

However long it takes.

By all accounts Bruce was free to move on and remarry, and with each uncertain year that he waited, he shortened his chances of having a family. But he still chose to hush the advice of the world and heed the prompting of his heart.

Cathy and Bruce were not alone in their struggle to live the single life God's way. They never considered themselves to have mastered obedience in their own strength; rather they had *been taken hold* of by Christ Jesus himself (Phil. 3:12) and chose to live according to his inspired truth.

They both allowed themselves to be a conduit of blessings for others. And just look at their rewards.

The mind is a sponge. Be discerning about
what it soaks up.

wise about good,
innocent about evil

chapter 13

I'm a nut for movies. My home office is plastered with classic movie posters—*Gone with the Wind, San Francisco, It's a Wonderful Life*—films made before I was born. I'm surrounded by Cary Grant, John Wayne, Clark Gable, and Elvis at his best. Scarlett eyes me in her shocking red dress, Dorothy clutches Toto, and Lucy is decked out like one of the Marx brothers. Bogart graces the opposite wall with his wistful, *Where did she come from?* gaze after he sees Ilsa stroll into his nightclub on her husband's arm. I can close my eyes and see him grumbling to Sam the piano player, "Of all the gin joints in all the towns in all the world, she walks into mine."

And I start humming "As Time Goes By."

Casablanca, Hollywood at its best, is a movie that never grows stale. It has all the ingredients—action, comedy, suspense, romance. The chaos of war, the sinister Nazis, the desperate refugees, the unrequited love of Rick and Ilsa and their unforgettable lament: "We'll always have Paris."

I watch it twice a year.

The American Film Institute rated *Casablanca* as the favorite love story of all time, and yet it's not about love at all. Legend tells us that the ending wasn't written until the last day, and Ingrid Bergman never knew which man she would choose, a bit unlikely considering the moral code of 1942 would never have allowed a married woman to dump her resistance-hero husband for the man she loves.

But it's a great legend.

It could have ended only one way for Rick—"I stick out my neck for nobody"—to sacrifice the woman he loves, to give her up for the higher good. His unforgettable words that show the rebirth to his ideals: "The problems of three little people don't amount to a hill of beans in this crazy world."

Movies have touched me and changed me. The producer of *Chariots of Fire* put into words my thoughts: "Far more than any other influence, more than school, more even than home, my attitudes, dreams, preconceptions and pre-conditions for life had been irreversibly shaped . . . in a place called Hollywood."[1]

Movies are a window through which God speaks, says author Ken Gire in *Windows of the Soul*. Film is a powerful art form because it reflects our longings, the deepest places in our soul, the longing that good triumphs over evil, that truth wins out, that life's dramas bring out the hero in us. A good character grows wiser, better, and more understanding, and a bad character, if not redeemed, is brought to justice.[2]

Movies don't always enlighten and inspire, he says, but we tend to lose ourselves, for the moment, in somebody else's story.

And it can be an epiphany of understanding.

He writes about movies that have taught him more lessons than college or seminary, movies like *Schindler's List*, *The Elephant Man*, *Camelot*, and *Shadowlands*.

We all have movie favorites that have allowed us to glimpse into worlds we would never otherwise know, and God speaks to us through these new landscapes. But for today's Christian theatergoer, the pickings are slim. So many movies are full of senseless sex and violence.

"Gratuitous violence," Carl reminds me. The "for kicks" kind—blood and guts without just cause. "Violence is not necessarily bad," he likes to tell me. "The Old Testament was full of it." Spoken by a true action flick guy. OK, I concede that one: violence has its cinematic place.

As a couple, we love the movie experience, from the trailers to the closing credits. We always stay seated quietly until the screen goes black and then head for Starbucks for a café mocha—a caramel macchiato for me—to dissect the movie and its message.

Because I'm a fan of musicals, *Chicago* was on my want-to-see list, so we joined another couple for an evening out. We all sat frozen for twenty minutes in the fifth row—we'd snuck in late—while dancers undulated to "All That Jazz." A spoof of the legal system of the 1920s, the guilty live happily ever after in a widescreen celebration of sin and naughtiness.

We all secretly wanted to walk out but didn't want to be the killjoy.

Some Christian friends raved about the top-notch acting, glitzy costumes, and fantastic musical numbers, and I agreed. Then I heard the dreaded question, "Well, how'd you like it?"

Stammer, stumble, trip over the tongue. "It made me . . . uncomfortable."

Pin-drop silence. Oops, am I now the prude, the holier-than-thou guardian of morality who can't look beyond a harmless fun-filled musical?

Paul told the church in Rome: "Be wise about what is good, yet innocent about what is evil" (Rom. 16:19).

Isn't that what God meant when he told Adam and Eve not to eat of a certain tree in the garden? They got exactly what they asked for, complete freedom to sample not only the sweet but also the sinister side of life, and we know how that turned out. Fig leaves and all.

Of late, before heading off to a flashy new ten-theater movie house in town, I have started checking reviews on Web sites that offer more than the premise of the film but how vulgar and offensive it is and how it might distress my spirit. More often we scrap our movie plans—nothing worth seeing—and call somebody up for a card game.

When *Cold Mountain* came out, it sounded like our type of movie, and in the middle of my book project, I neglected to check reviews. After all, it was a best-selling novel, though I had not yet read it. An R-rated film, which we rarely see but it must be the Civil War footage, I reasoned. Plus, Carl read me the *Sacramento Bee* review (that we seldom find reliable, so go figure): "Better than *Gone with the Wind.*"

"Book it, Danno," I told him. I still watch reruns of *Hawaii 5-0* on late night TV.

Squirming in our seats, we exchanged many glances. *This is not what we expected.*

That night we both woke up at two a.m., restless and disturbed. "I can't get the images out of my head," Carl said. Not the war scenes—war is expected to be bloody—but those in which the repulsive, sex-crazed, runaway preacher delights in an orgy with three stark naked women. I shielded my can't-believe-it eyes. Then it was the attempted rape scene by the vile Yankee soldiers, and the violent acts by the Southern home guard against their own people; hanging a woman on a fence after mercilessly slaughtering her family. Two-plus hours worth. Gratuitous violence because it seemed to be there just for shock value.

Why did we put ourselves through it? Why didn't we just walk out the minute our spirits were darkened? Because, in our optimism we waited for redemption, something that would put evil in its proper place and offer some kind of hope. Perhaps the women who fought to survive on the farm amid tragedy would draw solace and strength from their faith (Nicole Kidman's character was a minister's daughter), or if that's too far-fetched for Hollywood—and it was a script adapted from a book—at least a hint that good can emerge from tragedy.

Did I miss it?

"Why didn't you tell me you'd seen this movie?" my friend Judi gently demanded on the phone the next week. She described her almost perfect girls' day out with a close friend that ended with a movie. Unfortunately, *Cold Mountain* won the coin toss. The two had the same troubling reaction that we had.

Carl's late-night tussle over this movie led to several hours of morning conversation—and three cups of strong black tea for me—about the impact of the visual on the mind. "The mind is a powerful thing," Carl said, pouring his coffee. "It's like a sponge, absorbing everything. And some things are toxic. They can destroy us from the inside out."

So true. "A man is a slave to whatever has mastered him" (2 Pet. 2:19 NIV).

Now my husband knows all about my past, but not until this chat session—after his first bout with unwelcome images swirling in his head—did he grasp the reality of my statement, "They're still in my mind."

"They" meaning the porno movies my former husband asked me to watch over thirty years ago. A young bride eager to please my soldier home from Vietnam, I agreed. Suddenly, it swept me into a strange new world, and while my good girl side was repulsed, there was something hypnotic going on. I felt shamelessly titillated at the same time.

It was only two movies—I refused more—but two was enough to affect my sexuality for years to come. It was the end of my innocence.

Enough said. It never occurred to me that my first husband's search for sexual thrills outside the marriage had a connection to a swelling interest in pornography, but the clues were there from the girlie magazines hidden in the garage to his insatiable needs, which I knocked myself out to fill. Once he left me, I knew where my weak spot was. When Christ entered my life, and I finally admitted my powerlessness over temptation, I prayed for help bringing my thought life into obedience.

Not an easy task for a celibate single in the prime of my sexual life.

One restless midnight in a friend's home, I surfed the cable channels, and in what was probably a one-second pause, I viewed an explicit scene that titillated my senses and taunted me with impure thoughts.

Nonstop like a bullet train without a caboose.

I longed to give in to them, to lose myself in a fantasy (and those that have been there will understand), but I had lingered there once too often in my single life with a good dose of guilt for the finale. And a prayer and promise to God in all sincerity, one kept until some visual stimulus goaded me during one of my weak moments. Triggered by the usual things, stress and frustration over life's complexities.

I will forever be vulnerable, that I now know. I must guard the kind of visual images that come before me. There are those who would say, "So what? You're not committing any sin in those fantasies. You're not acting them out." We could spend pages looking at the views on this issue, from the relaxed to the restricted.

I can only speak for me and my temptations. Impure thoughts are self-centered, not God-centered. They transport me toward darkness, not light.

Long ago I discovered that feelings and cravings follow thoughts, and the answer to any temptation—anger, gossip, bitterness, food binges, and especially sexual—is to change those thoughts. Decide first not to place yourself in situations that feed them. We usually have the problems at certain times under similar conditions. Maybe late at night after a stressful day.

Alter those patterns in any way you can.

In those early days I had to give myself a mental shampoo almost every day. When a lustful X-rated thought roosted in my brain—usually in the dark, lonely midnight hours—I would sing my own version of a tune from South Pacific: "I'm gonna wash that thought right outta my brain . . . and send it on its way." I would envision it being sucked down the drain, swirling deep into the sewer.

Flushed clear out of my head. I still employ this tactic.

"We should wash ourselves clean from every impurity of the flesh and spirit" (2 Cor. 7:1), Paul told us. And give ourselves to God alone.

How many times have we heard that *though we walk in the flesh, we don't wage war in a fleshly way.* We're defenseless with our human weapons to fight the battles of the flesh. Whenever I threatened to leave my former mate, he won me over with a promise to get back into counseling. After a few months—with his sincere-at-the-time desire to change—we patched things up, and the counselor said, "You're good to go now."

We had him fooled, and ourselves. We just never got it. We were into changing behavior—his, mine, ours—but changing behavior never works except for the short run. We know that by the failure rate in twelve-step programs. As Dallas Willard reminds us in *Renovation of the Heart,* "Thoughts are the place where we can and must begin to change."[3]

Paul urges us to take every thought captive to the obedience of Christ (1 Cor. 10:5). And my pastor, who loves word pictures, illustrated it this way in a sermon: *Frisk every thought at the door.* Carl, the former police officer, can relate to this image. *Oops. Impure or lustful thought. Hand it over.*

I had to find my own word picture for this key verse. After complaining to my Internet server's help desk about excessive spam mail, I was informed about *block sender,* a nifty little click of the mouse on the suspecting e-mail causes a screen to pop up:

Subsequent messages from this sender will be blocked.

Now this little maneuver cannot possibly thwart the thousands of nuisance and evil spammers in cyberspace, but it's my own way of fighting back. As I assaulted a horde of them one morning, I thought to myself, *Satan is the ultimate spam sender, and though he assaults me daily, I have a weapon.*

Hot dog! I've got your number, devil. Don't mess with me. I'm wearing the armor of God.

Satan deluges us with garbage messages and tantalizing images—Internet pop-ups, sensual magazine ads, tantalizing prime-time television commercials, and when we're in voluntary captivity in a dark movie theater eager to lose ourselves in someone else's story.

While these tactics pertain to most temptations, our modern blight remains pornography. The number using it is nearly as high as those who aren't, according to Donna Rice Hughes, a champion in the fight against illegal pornography. She adds that one in six women, including Christian women, are struggling with online porn addiction.[4]

I can understand how this curse can possess you, one peek at a time.

Carl and I renewed our vow not to muddy up our minds at the movies. So will we keep buying mainstream movie tickets? Yes, but only as prudent consumers, and we're inviting Jesus to every showing to keep us accountable. As my friend Cecil Murphey says, it's not something you can explain; it's your own personal encounter with the voice that brings conviction.

It's the touch of the Holy.

We recently rented a movie guaranteed to bring chuckles, some church friends said. A sparkling screwball romantic comedy, supposedly, and one of 2003's hit movies. An aging playboy whose only goal in life is to sleep with young women is nearly in bed with one when her mother arrives at their beach house. The man soon has a heart attack, and while convalescing, the playboy and mother fall in love. In the classic movie days, he would have been a pervert; but now he's quite the catch, only slightly misguided.

Beside the brief nudity and language, the movie was one lust scene after the other, and most of the talk centered on sex. The stars' first sexual encounter was "laugh-out-loud funny," so said a reviewer, but halfway through I sensed that familiar tug that translates, "This isn't comfortable for you," and turned it off.

Is it the prude side of me again? *Come on, just a little harmless fun. Don't be so uptight.*

I'm grateful for a God who knows me so intimately, who understands the bondage of my past and how desperately I need Philippians 4:8: "Whatever is true, whatever is honorable, and whatever is just, whatever is pure, whatever is lovely, whatever is commendable—if there is any moral excellence and if there is any praise—dwell on these things."

Watching Mel Gibson during his interview about his controversial movie with Diane Sawyer on *Primetime*, I wondered if the spiritual bankruptcy he spoke of—that caused him to abuse alcohol and drugs—had any connection to his disenchantment with some of the shameless products spewing out of Hollywood. He once contemplated hurling himself out of a window. Instead, he turned to the Bible and began to meditate on the Gospels.

And *The Passion of the Christ* was born.

We saw it on opening night, a brutal film, and the graphic images were agonizing to watch, yet I needed to be "sent to the edge" as Gibson puts it, to understand Paul's words, "I resolved to know nothing . . . except Jesus Christ and him crucified" (1 Cor. 2:2 NIV).

The controversial epic tells more than the story of Christ's last day; it is the tale of a successful actor who "had it all" and found it empty, who cried out in despair to God and then followed his call to make a film about Jesus, a film using two dead languages, with no known stars, and a script straight out of the Gospel. Financing it himself, he endured attacks and criticism and followed through on his commitment.

And look what God has done with his obedience. My friend Roanne sent an e-mail the morning after she saw it. "Wow! I agree with you. It wasn't a movie; it was an experience! I was emotionally beat when we left the theater. We were all stunned. I am so glad to have been able to see it. It left me with so much more reverence for what Jesus endured and wanting to know so much more. Awesome! All of a sudden I feel like I can't get enough."

Movies are powerful forces.

In *Casablanca* freedom fighter Victor Laszlo told Rick, "Each of us has a destiny, for good and evil." He was talking about the choices we make. And if we keep making the wrong ones, ignoring our conscience, the heart can become so insensitive to evil that over time it grows insensitive to God.

If movies are a window through which God speaks, they are more than just entertainment; they are ways in which God throws light on his truth and reaches us with new understanding. Paul understood this when he told Timothy to hold on to his faith and *good conscience*.

Our inner twinges—the confirming voice of a caring God. An obedient heart welcomes them.

right angle:
the God's eye view

chapter 14

Time magazine called her the "party crasher"—Sherron Watson, the gutsy woman who spoke up and broke up the giant corporation that paid her salary.

You may recall when Enron collapsed while the world looked on.

Sherron, who served as vice president in accounting, at first hesitated to confront senior management with her discovery of the company fraud. She decided to seek counsel, not from an attorney or a business ethics manual, but from her pastor and Bible study group friends. Convinced she was doing the right thing, she took the risk and stepped forward. What began with an in-house memo outlining her concerns exploded into national headlines.

Sharon never set out to be a whistle blower at all; she was just doing her job. Suddenly she was the toast of America. She joined the ranks of Charles Lindberg, Winston Churchill, Ronald Reagan, and the Pope to become one of *Time* magazine's Persons of the Year.

But as her Sunday school teacher told *World Magazine*, her friends sometimes wondered, *What's the big deal? She is only doing what a Christian ought to do.*[1]

But it's a foreign concept to a world without Christ.

In a national survey adults were asked this question: "Do you believe there are moral absolutes—unchanging truths—or are moral truths relative to the circumstances." Three to one, the answer was: *Truth is always relative to the person and the situation.*

And the answers weren't all from non-Christians; many were professed believers. The difference, the researcher noted, was nothing to cheer about. Many believers today are blindly casting their vote for what is dubbed as *moral relativism* or *situation ethics.*

Where do we get the "if it feels good, do it," "everyone else is doing it" and "as long as it doesn't hurt anyone else" philosophies that are so contrary to God's way?

That's a good question.

I relate it to one of my first wallpapering experiences at our house. Carl suggested I wait until the weekend when he'd be glad to help, but I opted to go it alone. After gathering all the materials, sizing the walls, measuring and cutting the paper strips, I started at the logical place, a corner. The first few strips went up without a hitch, no unsightly air bubbles. But, before long the strips wouldn't match up anymore without major crimping. I stood back and saw my dilemma.

Oops. The corner must not have been square, and my first strip was a hair off center. The gap widened with each new one. The whole room soon leaned to the left. Too bad I didn't know about a magic device called a plumb line, a small heavy weight hanging from a cord with handy purple chalk you pull to make sure the starting spot is straight.

Or a level, which Carl told me later is what he always uses.

It would have saved the day. It took twice as long to rip, remove, and repair my botched job. Not to mention the money for new paper that had to be purchased by the double roll.

Whether you need it or not.

When we find ourselves agreeing with the world's opinions and not God's, it's time to pause and reflect and see if our viewpoint is a bit distorted.

In a vision the prophet Amos saw the Lord measure the nation of Israel with a plumb line (Amos 7:7–8). God always conveys a message with images familiar to our life and times. For the Jews at this moment in their history, it was locusts, fire, and a plumb line. The nifty little tool pops up again in Isaiah 28:17, "I will make . . . righteousness the plumb line" (NIV).

When our attitudes, beliefs, values, and opinions line up with God's, we naturally adopt the Christian worldview.

When Sherron Watkins faced her difficult decision, she drew on what she knew to be the truth. Not her views or a collection of opinions but what God's Word says. By turning a blind eye to what was going on in her company, she would be partnering in corruption.

"Do not let my heart turn to any evil thing or wickedly perform reckless acts with men who commit sin. Do not let me feast on their delicacies" (Ps. 141:4).

Though it was obvious the company would take a dive, Sherron took the high road, not only giving up her $165,000-a-year job, but opting not to dump her stock and bank on her integrity instead.

When I read the book *Born Again* by Chuck Colson,[2] I saw the same thing. Not yet forty, the ex-marine captain was appointed special counsel to President Nixon and soon became known as the "hatchet man," who stated, "I would walk over my grandmother if necessary to assure the President's reelection."

Then the Watergate scandal hit in 1973, and he was in big trouble. A friend gave him C. S. Lewis's *Mere Christianity*, and he saw himself as a man of pride who had destroyed his life.[3] Soon after, he offered himself wholly to God.

Colson was accused of knowing about the Watergate break-in—a crime of which he was innocent—but he was guilty of something else, obstruction of justice. He had helped spearhead the illegal wiretapping of Democratic headquarters.

What a choice. Keep silent and be acquitted; speak up and go to prison.

"Who may ascend the hill of the LORD? Who may stand in his holy place? He who has clean hands and a pure heart" (Ps. 24:3–4 NIV).

Colson confessed his crime and professed his faith publicly all at once. The skeptics wondered if the "hatchet man's" conversion was genuine. One reporter commented, "If Mr. Colson can repent of his sins, there just has to be hope for everybody."

He hit that one right on target.

Colon's behind-bars experience altered his life, leading him to found the nonprofit Prison Fellowship Ministries after his release in 1976, funded with royalties from his book. When he found Christ, Colson's attitudes and values became God's, and while his decisions were still difficult, he had a holy plumb line with which to square them.[4]

My husband Carl has no such dramatic story, but he measures all his choices by the plumb line of righteousness. That's why he attracted me. After a few years of marriage, he had difficulty sleeping. "It's living with me," I joked, which was not so far-fetched. Because we'd both given up our "real" jobs for self-employment—he urged me to quit working at the capitol and follow my writing dream—Carl felt under pressure to juggle the finances. And send me to conferences, update my computer, and whatever else a serious freelance writer would need.

The problem continued for three years, and we searched for a physical cause. Our doctor prescribed some mild sleeping pills and finally sent him to a sleep clinic for further study. Meanwhile, Carl, who has never had any medical issues and has the healthy heart of a twenty-year-old, according to his last doctor, applied for a life insurance policy to give me a cushion, just in case something happened to him.

The application stated: *Are you on any medication? What kind?* Time out for a confession: I popped out with, "Why even bother mentioning it on the application? You won't be on the pills for more than a few weeks anyway, knowing your distaste for drugs." At that moment Carl was ingesting one little pill at night, so his answer had to be yes.

Oops! Sleeping pills are a red flag to insurance companies. *Could be severe emotional problems.* They would approve the policy but at a premium 25 percent higher than the original quote. As soon as he went off the drug—sixty days later as it turned out—Carl could reapply but would have to wait eighteen months to decrease the premium.

Telling the truth can be costly at any level.

But Carl didn't care. "I have my integrity. That's worth more than elevated cost." Case closed.

We faced the same scenario when it came to adding on to our existing deck at the cabin. *Bumblebee Summer Home Tract,* twenty-one rustic cabins built in the late forties, sits on Forest Service (USFS) land that we lease by lot from the government. Since we bought our place when it was in shambles and went right to work renovating it, our neighbors were generous with the horror stories about the way the Forest Service operates. Neighbors had tried to do everything "by the book" and found nothing but hassles, so their advice became, "Oh, just slap it up quick. It's easier to get forgiveness than permission."

Not Carl. He insisted we do it right, get a proper building permit, and make application to the local USFS office. "The rules may be unfair and archaic," Carl said, "but somebody somewhere is watching every move we make because they know we're Christ followers."

That's my guy. "The question is," he added, "how much are you willing to sell your integrity for?"

As predicted, it turned out to be a nightmare, costing twice what we budgeted and taking two years longer to complete. Though it was overbuilt and would outlast us, the contractor had it engineered for another county's snow load requirements, so we almost had to tear it all down. But God rescued the project at the last minute when the building inspector made a personal visit and must have liked us. "I'll sign it like it is," he said.

So each summer we relax in our Adirondack chairs on our deck shaded by lofty fir trees and watch stellar jays scoop up sunflower seeds off the railing, content that we honored God with our actions. I now have a greater understanding of what "the fear of the LORD is the beginning of wisdom" (Ps. 111:10) really means.

God says, "I'll turn conventional wisdom on its head" (1 Cor. 1:19 *The Message*). And he does it through believers willing to risk a personal loss or setback to stand for him.

Our Christian worldview is akin to the difference between a visit to the optometrist and just grabbing a pair of "cheaters" at the drugstore to get you by. Without a customized prescription to correct the eyesight, things might seem clear, but they are not in perfect focus. We just think they are.

Last fall Pat Nolan came out to Sacramento as the featured speaker for a pregnancy center fund-raiser, and I hadn't seen him since he left the capitol for prison nine years before. Poking at my prime rib dinner, I concentrated on every word from a man whose life and work so affirm the reality of a redeeming God. *His way of thinking is so different*, I thought, from the old legislative days when his traditional Catholic faith was merely a backup when common sense had a question.

His worldview had completely changed. *Worldview* is a catch-phrase used to describe our belief system, the way we see the world and form our decisions. We live in a casual society today where people tout, "That may be true for you, but it's not true for me."

What we deem is right comes straight out of our worldview. Last year the Barna Group studied churches and reported that 90 percent of church and lay leaders have no understanding of what it means to have a Christian worldview. Chuck Colson wonders if it's not our move from the *Word-driven message* to an *entertainment-driven* message.

Whatever the cause, I agree with Barna who says, "The reason people don't act like Jesus, is because they don't think like Jesus."[5]

Once God's holiness becomes our measuring stick, we adopt scriptural values. There's no juggling the question of whether to lie about our child's age to get the Disneyland discount, agree to fudge on the sales price of a private party car purchase to save on the transfer fee tax, or build the deck without getting the required permits. No shortcuts considered.

To stand firm in obedience, we must filter every decision through the lens of God's reputation and ask ourselves this: Will what I'm about to do advance the cause of Christ or hurt it? That's kingdom living at its best.

John Wayne as Davy Crockett in the 1960 film epic *The Alamo*, drawled this: "There's right and there's wrong. You got to do one or the other. You do the one and you're living. You do the other and you may be walking around, but you're dead as a beaver hat."

Probably the Texas paraphrase of James 4:17: "So, for the person who knows to do good and doesn't do it, it is a sin."

The by-product of the right choice is a spiritual jackpot that keeps paying off.

Have a right relationship with money.
God owns it all anyway.

king's ransom

chapter 15

A part from God, life is like slowly starving on a desert island. You've got the king's ransom in gold stacked up on the beach, but it's worthless because it can't buy what you really need.

Money is the ultimate plumb line, one of the most accurate measures of how our priorities line up with God's. It's a test of where he rates in our lives. We give in proportion to how much we love.

Jay discovered this when he first met Christ. "I'd survived a tour in Vietnam with only a passing thought about God. Once home I signed on to play in a citywide baseball league. I met a Christian pastor who kept bugging me to come to his church. To shut him up, I went. And God hit me between the eyes.

"He stepped on me big time," Jay said with a laugh. "I had been spending my money on all the wrong things—partying, smoking, drinking. I gave it all up and started tithing when I realized how much God loved me."

Overnight he faced a jungle more challenging than Southeast Asia. His wife left, and on top of the emotional upheaval, he had three young ones to support—five, four, and eighteen months.

"She never helped out financially," Jay said. "I wondered how I'd juggle the child care costs. I was determined to keep the kids and make it work. Still, I just kept tithing, giving 10 percent off the top—out of obedience—and I'm so bad with money. I never had a budget and never balanced my checkbook."

I chuckled at his candid confession. I'm checkbook-balance challenged myself and adhere to the philosophy that "close enough is good enough." Jay met me for an impromptu lunch interview at La Bou after I put out the call during Sunday school for obedience stories, and over hearty vegetable soup he told me his story.

In all the years he raised the kids alone—Jay is newly an empty nester and still single—he never sent a house payment in late or carried credit card debt for more than a month. "I made sure the kids were in church every Sunday, and every Sunday I wrote my weekly check. That's what I'd promised God I'd do."

Five years into his solo parenthood, he opened his home to a guest pastor who was teaching a financial seminar at church. "Have you ever had a financial analysis done, Jay?" he was asked.

"I was just a meat cutter. I could barely spell *analysis*. The only numbers I ever juggled were in ounces and pounds. But if this guy wanted to work out a budget for me, great."

After running the calculator for an hour, the pastor raised his perplexed head. "Jay, I don't know how long you've been operating like this, but you have $300 more in bills than salary."

That was worth a big grin. "It was obvious God was taking good care of us."

As the kids grew, so did Jay's expenses. "They didn't have a mom, so I wanted them to enjoy all the activities they wanted." I decided to work a few Sundays for some extra cash.

It seemed right at the time, just a temporary measure. *I'll get back to church soon.* But *soon* turned into three years. "Three years without worshipping God with my church family. Three years without giving God my time or money. The months just got away from me. I kept telling myself I still loved him, and my circumstances couldn't be helped."

We are so good at rationalizing, aren't we?

Then came the onslaught of financial problems. "There I was with a fistful of maxed-out credit cards, playing the switching game, paying one off with another one for six months of cheaper interest. It was crazy. High-stress time."

And then came his crisis: heart bypass surgery. "I was mad at God. How could he let this happen to me?"

We blame God for many things he has no part in, Jay admits. "I should have been dead, so the doctors told me. What a wake-up call. After everything the Lord had done for me, and I pointed the finger at him for my troubles? What nerve. I'm the one who wasn't going to church, wasn't studying and reading the Word. I'm the one who wasn't following through on promises made. I'm the one who shifted positions, not him."

One Sunday morning more than a year ago, Jay showed up in our Sunday school class. *I know that guy*, I thought and searched back to the past. Yes, he used to be buddies with my next-door—a quarter mile through the woods—neighbor in Greenwood, but since he had little ones to raise and mine were almost teens—he started his day late and I started early—we connected only briefly. Now I observed him as a man steadfast in his faith. And my female brain started calculating: *Which one of my still-single gal pals might I hook him up with?* OK, it's hard to give up the old matchmaker tricks. Best to leave Jay to his own timetable.

He is debt-free again and living what he calls the "all or nothing" life with God, giving off the top of his income with no reservations. When he travels, he makes sure his tithe gets to church before he does. And this man travels whenever he can. "There's always money to do it, and no—I still don't balance my checkbook."

We need to see money as a gift we give back to God, Jay says, for no other reason than this: because we love him. "Why play tug-of-war with our money; God owns it all anyway."

Janet and Jim stumbled onto this truth in a similar way, and when I heard their short testimony during the pastor's once-a-year sermon on giving—and he does a great job with a difficult subject—I jotted a note: *Chat with them about it for my book.*

"We were upside down in our house," Jim admitted later. "We'd borrowed on it to landscape the yard, then redo all the windows, and update the appliances. The warning signs were all there, but we didn't listen."

"We wanted the good life," added Janet. "I bought things because, well, . . . I deserved them, and let's face it, we like our stuff. Buying makes us feel good."

When the going gets tough, the tough go shopping. I said that already, didn't I?

Though Jim had a secure position with a grocery store in town, they were too far behind on payments to save the house, and the bank foreclosed. "If you've ever gone through it, you know the humiliation, the sense of failure," he said. "And all the questions you ask yourself about why and how it happened."

Self-examination time. "We'd been Christians for almost twenty years, *when it suited us*," Janet piped up. "There we were in our little rented house, knowing we had to start over in every way. That meant getting ourselves to church every Sunday."

Meanwhile, Jim quit his grocery job. "I'd been wanting to make a change for a while, to start my own business. Now that we were getting our priorities in order, it seemed the right time to follow my heart."

Have mop will travel. Jim put out the word that he had gone into the housecleaning business. "People looked down at him," Janet said. "He'd be going out to the designer homes of the wealthy doctors and lawyers in town to give them a bid on cleaning toilets. They'd look at him like, *'Poor guy, he must be really bad off if he has to resort to this.'*"

Jim has never been happier in his life.

One morning in church, when the offering bag was about to come by, Janet noticed her husband reach into his wallet for a check. "What's this?" she demanded and snatched it out of his hand. Dumbfounded at the amount, she growled as quietly as possible, "We'll talk about this later."

"No, we won't." Jim stuffed it inside the bag.

As they drove out of the parking lot, the conversation heated up. "I was so angry at him," Janet said. "I had no idea he'd been tithing, 10 percent right off the top, side jobs and everything. I wondered how we were ever going to get back on our feet if we gave *that much* to the church. It just didn't make sense to me."

It's always tempting to shortchange God. We think he doesn't need it like we do, Janet added later. "We'd been almost possessed by a house, caught in an endless cycle of wanting more and better." Hearing this reminded me of 1 Timothy 6:10: "For the love of money is a root of all kinds of evil, and by craving it, some have wandered away from the faith and pierced themselves with many pains."

But Janet gave in. "And that was my beginning, when I let God completely change my heart. You know the verse, 'a fool [is] wise in his own eyes' (Prov. 26:5 NIV). I had it all wrong. It wasn't about me and what I thought was right. Jim was head of the household, and above all, I needed to honor and obey him, which is the same as honoring and obeying Christ. For me, it was about giving up control. I'm such a control freak," she said with a smile.

Within three years, working as a team, their income quadrupled. They wondered, would owning another home be possible now? "But nobody would lend us any money, not with our credit," Janet said. "But we were still content." And then the miracle happened—the details aren't important—but they found a piece of rural property with a modest house on it, and the financing fell into place. "Something only God could do. He restored everything we'd lost and more. And yet that's not a reason to give to God; it's just a by-product of the right attitude about money."

Jim and Janet serve on the deacon board at our church. "I listen to God now," Janet made sure to tell me, and I wrote it down on my notes. "I used to listen to God only after things fell apart. Now it's his agenda, not ours."

Donna and Dave's story is a parallel. As a young couple, they were risk takers; and when Dave's friend lured them with, "There's a ton of money to be made down here," they sold everything, packed their two youngsters in the car, and headed south to Mexico.

"We worked like crazy seven days a week, but it was a disaster," Donna said. "Our partner was doing things that were unethical, yet we were sucked in by the lure of fast cash." Donna, who had come to Christ several years before while Dave was still a prebeliever, was desperate for answers. She found a tight-knit group of Christians and joined them for Bible study. "I had never tithed. *What a terrible thing—for the church to ask us for money,* I thought. Oh, once in a while I'd give ten dollars and think I was so generous."

Getting into God's Word opened her eyes, especially Malachi. "Tithing isn't a suggestion. It's a command, I learned." Dave was not on the same page. "But we have nothing to tithe," he argued. A fact that didn't deter Donna, who decided on her own to give back to God. "Lord, I don't understand this," she prayed, "and I am not the least bit joyful about it, but if this is what we're supposed to do, I'm complying."

For extra money Donna baked and sold bread, and 10 percent came right off the top. Often, it was the only cash they had. "When it hurts, that's what tithing is all about." Their business venture flopped—wrong choice of partner Donna says, plus worldly decisions with no thought of God's ways—and their nest egg had vanished.

They came back to California broke but wiser. "The first thing we did was find a church," Donna said, which is where we met this couple. "Then we looked for jobs. Suddenly, I could hardly wait to write the tithe check. I began to feel the joy in giving. It filled my whole soul." And very soon God began blessing their finances, big time.

Dave took notice of this strange and wonderful way that God works, and when a group of men carpooled to a Promise Keepers event, Dave tagged along. "And I came home totally broken, my heart and eyes opened to the Lord."

And did God surprise Donna. "I envisioned myself the martyr for the rest of my life married to him, never sharing faith together."

And she credits it all to her obedience with giving. "Once I got that down, everything else seemed easy. Once I put God in charge of my finances, he took over every other part of my life."

Always a generous person, Donna's motivation took a U-turn. "I used to give and wait for the pat on the back. '*Oh, isn't she nice?*' I wanted them to see Donna. Now I want people to see *Jesus through Donna.*"

Dave and Donna now have more than enough money. Donna calls it the holy multiplication table. "I've started this little tradition," she said. "When I write the giving check, I put a happy face next to the amount. It isn't just another obligation, another bill to be paid; it's my love note to God. *You are the generous Giver of all things.*"

Each of these friends has learned that what we earn is not really ours, and we should return a portion to the God we love as a present, a gift. If you look up *gift* in the dictionary, it's defined as an "unsolicited repayment." Out of gratitude and recognition for what he's done for us, we give back to him. The amount is not the key, but our attitude.

The Israelites had the tithing thing all wrong. There were legalists who obeyed the law thinking their obedience would earn them righteousness before God, and there were those who shrugged off the command altogether—better things to do with the money—and deprived the temple storehouse of what it needed to keep going.

According to some statistics, only one out of every ten born-again believers sets aside 10 percent of their income for God. If we're stingy about giving God our money, we rob ourselves of the spiritual blessings.

The prophet Malachi, whose book is a bridge between the Old and New Testaments, told the Jews that in robbing God they were robbing themselves. "Bring the whole tithe into the storehouse. . . . Test me in this . . . and see if I will not throw open the floodgates of heaven and pour out so much blessing that you will not have room . . . for it" (Mal. 3:10 NIV).

I know this is true. Yet I can relate to the rich young ruler who balked at Jesus telling him to sell everything he owned (Luke 18:18–29). *Get rid of everything that's more important than God,* he was told, but he couldn't do it. He chose to walk away, very sad. I gulp when I read this parable. Because of my emotional, insecure past, money became a safety net for me for years. Only recently have I loosened my grip on it. Giving is now on its way to being the joy it's meant to be.

Jeanne overheard me asking for anecdotes about money for this book and offered this little story about having the right attitude toward money. She was buying a local newspaper, and when she dropped in her quarter, out slid thirteen dollars more—just like a slot machine. "I marched right into the *Auburn Journal* office and gave it all back to them. Of course, they were in awe. People just don't do that. At the time I thought: *I could really use this money,* but right is right."

That Christian worldview in action again.

The same week her checking account showed zero. Jeanne is single and a teacher. She doesn't get a paycheck for two months in the summer. "I didn't even have enough for milk. But as I was doing my laundry, I reached into the pocket of my shorts, and there was a twenty-dollar bill."

Yes, Lord, this is your principle.

Obedience doesn't always come with such immediate reward; often it delays for a long time, but true wealth is never logged in any bank account. Jesus told his disciples that anyone who sacrifices for him gets it back a hundred times over and a bonus of eternal life besides.

Sounds like a worthy profit-sharing program, a heavenly one at that. Sign me up.

Obedience helps us look beyond a tough
situation to God's purposes whether we
understand them or not.

low tide, higher ground

chapter 16

Tressa, my Bible study friend from chapter 1, married her childhood sweetheart for one pressing reason: to keep him from being drafted and sent to Vietnam. Not the most sensible motivation for marriage, but if you were young in those crazy days of flower children, campus unrest, racial riots, sex, drugs, and rock and roll, you'd understand the decision to "make love not war."

Those were the days when marriage meant armed forces deferment, and when it came to Uncle Sam, you were guaranteed an unlisted number. I recently contacted Tressa in Southern California to refresh me about her story. "It's hard to remember back that far, so this can get fuzzy, Jan," she warned.

What she does remember with clarity is their separation a few short years after their son Peter was born. "I hoped Miko would come to his senses and want to make the marriage work, for our young son's sake at least, but to hush the advice givers in my family who insisted I protect myself, I bought a do-it-yourself divorce book. Since I'm lazy—as you well know—I never pursued it."

And neither did Miko.

Years later, when Peter found Christ through a local youth group, he hounded his mother until she joined him at church, just when her soul was ready to embrace Christ. And she'll never forget how God spoke plainly to her heart. "For me there was Miko only, and if he was to turn his life to Christ, he would be the husband I wanted. If that did not happen, and God wanted me to be with someone else, then he'd just have to send Miko to his grave. I was not going to sever the marriage ties."

Tressa wouldn't budge. "Or wish for something different for my life or even allow myself to think about it or live in regret."

But then came the onslaught of criticism. "You must not have normal sexual needs. Could there be something *wrong* with you?"

Something wrong with following God?

It was her first experience with being hassled for what she felt was an act of obedience, one strictly between her and her Lord, and she was not about to justify or explain it. "Satan was trying to get me off track through insensitive believers. Miko proved as lazy as I am—something we share in common—and he's never pursued a divorce in all these years. It's a protection of sorts for him, I think, but I've come to see it as God's unique plan for us."

As she began to use her gifts in ministry at her local church, one pastor questioned her marital situation, but she responded with conviction, "He is the husband of my youth."

With her signature dry humor, she asks, "Would they have blinked twice if I had been divorced and remarried? Would they have dug into the details to make certain it was biblical? I doubt it."

In this day and age, it's strange to be in Tressa's situation, to have no interest in finalizing papers and *moving on.* "Paul tells the Corinthians that each should remain in the situation he was in when God called him, and for me that's living alone while still legally married," she said. "I have never had an interest in another relationship, thus no reason to divorce. It has greatly simplified my life. My purpose on earth is to serve God, and that's what I'm doing."

I can attest to that. Tressa is a perfect fit for junior high ministry. She has the time to spend and a knack for loving these kids at their most awkward age. When Amy was in her pre-prodigal years, I struggled relating to her, but never Tressa.

"She's very cool, Mom," Amy told me after a youth group meeting one night. *And I'm not?* I wanted to say, but I already knew the answer. It's hard to be cool when you're walking on hot bricks trying to be both mom and dad.

Presently, Tressa and Miko are the best of friends. Their son Peter is getting married this month, and she told me with a snicker, "I spent hours on the phone with Miko today. Ma and Pa Kettle are struggling with *what to wear* issues."

If you knew easy-going, unconventional Tressa, who seldom steps out of her Birkenstocks, you'd chuckle as I'm doing now just thinking of her trying to prepare for her mother-of-the-groom moment.

Not only does she have no regrets for her decision to remain faithful to God's call, she is one of the most satisfied people I know and never stresses about the future. "Obedience is definitely spiritually rewarding," she said. Twenty-two years after our 3-D Bible study, she is still an encouragement to me.

So is Amanda. I first met this gal when we were about to share a double bed at a conference. "I'm quiet, and I don't snore," she said. "I'm the perfect bunkmate." True, and as a bonus she stocked the mini-fridge with carrots, apples, and trail mix.

I liked her right off. We stayed up past midnight munching and sharing our stories. Her nightmare began when her I-can-do-anything husband had a stroke. She believed he'd be miraculously healed. "And we'd give God the glory. I kept repeating what I thought were Job's words, 'Though he slay me, yet will I praise him.' I refused to give up."

Reality set in when their income dwindled, and Tony didn't improve. He said partial paralysis, and his mental powers were almost gone. His keen wit had disappeared. "I couldn't care for Tony, the house, the farm, and the Arabian horses we raised. The thought of living with this man for the rest of my life was intolerable. He was only a shell of the man I once knew."

My locust years seemed like a clam dig compared to this.

For two years she struggled, bitter over what had happened to Tony. "I began to think we'd both be better off dead. Maybe I could smother him with a pillow when he was asleep. I was so filled with rage but stuffed it. I wanted him to die. I kept thinking, *Divorce is not an option, but murder is.*"

"Wow." I plucked a few raisins out of the trail mix and asked, "How did you resolve it?"

"I finally admitted I needed help. I saw a counselor twice a week who let me talk, cry, and wail. I had a decision to make: forgive Tony—I blamed him for messing it all up: no more travel, no more horse farm, all our dreams destroyed—and accept my new life or stay depressed and bitter at God. This was my crisis of faith. And then I thought of Tony, lying there in a bed so depressed because he couldn't even communicate his pain."

She reread Job 13:15 (KJV) and found what it actually says, "Though he slay me, yet will I *trust* in him." The Holman CSB version says it this way, "Even if He *kills* me, I will hope in Him. . . . *This will result in my deliverance.*"

Deliverance, restoration, reconstruction—it's all one and the same. And that's what Amanda received after she yielded the situation to God, after she determined to embrace the right attitude toward her situation.

When Tony improved, they traded the farm for life in a retirement village where he has a social life in the community. Though still partially paralyzed on the left side, they are content with life. "The time I spend with Tony is again a joy."

And Tony gets out every day to take his dog to the nursing home. "To visit people less fortunate than me," he says. He also started a "helpful hands" ministry, devising inventions to help stroke victims who only have the use of one hand.

Amanda, with no barns to muck and horses to groom, took up writing on a whim. She enrolled in some writing and speaking classes, and when we met, she had submitted her story to *Today's Christian Woman* and was about to get her first book contract. "Who would have ever dreamed? You know, Jan, getting my way is no longer my priority. How blind I was. God has purposes beyond what we can see."

Isn't that the recurring theme for so many stories, new and old? Life's toughest situations bring out the best in people.

That happened for Carmen when her second marriage became the nightmare she always feared. Her husband Dave came down with Huntington's Disease (HD), a hereditary disorder of the central nervous system. "He was sick when he married me, though he didn't know it was HD, and he chose to lie about his health."

The unforgivable sin for Carmen. As he quickly declined, she cared for him but rarely spoke. "I told him with contempt that I had to sort things out and couldn't be around him until I was ready." Her friends were free with advice. "The vast majority were appalled, urging me to find a nursing home for him, get a divorce, and begin my life again. The temptation was never far from my mind."

But it wasn't the right thing to do. Carmen prayed God would help her forgive Dave. In time she came to see her own shortcomings. "There is nothing I can do that God won't forgive me for the first time I ask him. Dave was a desperately sick man with a disease that already had begun to rob him of his faculties. He made a mistake, but did that mean he deserved abandonment? If I chose to walk away, God would still love and forgive me, but would that be the right thing to do? At that instant I forgave him and recommitted myself to give him the best care he deserved."

For years Carmen saw to Dave's immediate needs until she had to put him in a care facility. She has never been sorry. Through self-surrender she learned to understand grace.

"I would not be the person I am today if I had not made that choice."

Nor would Deb, who flourished in her job as an office manager in a small advertising firm. "My boss appreciated my work and was a great emotional support, but he was unhappily married. I always encouraged him to try to work things out with his wife," she told me. "We had a great platonic relationship. I never felt threatened, and he never did or said anything to indicate that I was anything more to him than one of the best employees he'd ever had."

Until she came back from maternity leave. He let his intentions be known. She confided in her husband, who agreed she should work only during regular business hours to play it safe. But her boss found ways to persist, so she made the difficult choice of resigning her position.

"We'll manage," her husband told her. "You're doing the right thing."

"I had mixed feelings. Obedience is hard. Sometimes in the middle of the night, I cried. On the one hand, I was relieved because it was the right thing, and I was victorious over temptation. But I was angry that my conscience was so tender that I had to quit a job that so perfectly fit my lifestyle. It was years before I saw any tangible fruit of my obedience, and that was difficult.

"Years later when I faced a similar but greater temptation, I saw that because of past victories I had developed spiritual muscle. That's the major lesson to learn from my story. Obeying God isn't something that brings instant rewards with warm fuzzy feelings.

"Yet God loves us and has plans for us, plans to prosper us and make us whole," Deb added. Some of those plans include tough workouts, and our spiritual muscles ache after exercise. Building spiritual muscles takes the same effort as building physical muscles. And you never know when those muscles will be *vital* to your survival. You have to be faithful in doing the workouts and trust that God will be faithful on his end.

God doesn't want outward obedience,

but a true change of heart.

pharisees and phylacteries

chapter 17

Tear your hearts, not just your clothes, and return to the LORD your God" (Joel 2:13). It's what the prophet Joel told the Jews after the locusts devoured everything green and brought on drought and devastation. These biblical folks were pros at clothes shredding, the public display of shame and deep remorse for sin and disobedience. Yet for many it had become another religious ritual. Mourn loud enough and God will surely hear and respond.

Another version states, "Rend your heart, and not your garments" (KJV), and Joel was saying simply this: Give up rolling in the dust and get right with God. Go beyond verbally confessing and mourning for your mistakes and lost opportunities, and make ragged your heart, rip it to shreds over your sin—your spiritual apathy—and come back to God.

He alone is the force to be reckoned with, not armies of insects. They are only the instruments he is using to prod you into obedience.

We all have locusts in our lives, giant wake-up calls, reminders to check the status of our plumb line.

I'm so good at going through the motions. I breeze into church with a sunshine smile and welcome the visitors. I perform all the visuals, raise my hands in passionate worship, kneel at the edge of the stage for our "garden of prayer," listen intently to the sermon and make notes in my journal, highlight important passages in the Bible, drop the tithe check into the offering bag, and take communion. To those around me I must appear the mature and faithful Christian.

But am I—or is it a bit of a show sometimes? Have I entered the sanctuary with a teachable spirit, or is my defensive shield in place? It's so easy to go through the motions assuming God is pleased, without letting his Word penetrate the heart and prick the conscience. Without asking, "Search me, God, and know my heart; test me and know my concerns. See if there is any offensive way in me; lead me in the everlasting way" (Ps. 139:23–24).

Offensive simply means "unacceptable to God."

Not long ago, Carl and I woke up early—four a.m.—and had one of our spur-of-the-moment, under-the-blanket talks until six. "I'm wondering," he said, thinking aloud, "if after my second term is up at the end of the year, I should resign the elder board. I've done what God called me to do, and it may be time to step down." Carl spearheaded the forming of our first church bylaws and served as our first elder chair. I felt my lips pucker and blurted, "But I like being an elder's wife."

He gave me that one-eyed puzzled look. "And why is that?"

A bayonet of truth made its first slice, forcing me to examine this insight. I've been proud of Carl as he used his gifts as a vital part of our church, but the stinging truth is that I like *telling* people I'm an elder's wife. Instant identification as a leader—leader's spouse, almost the same thing—the crème de la crème of the church.

Sounds a tad pharisaical and self-righteous, don't you think? I never considered myself as an image seeker, not until that dawning moment when Carl pondered leaving the board to become just a regular servant. Yikes—no more being "in the know" at church? Or jumping out of my seat when the pastor says, "Elders and their wives will be up front after the service for prayer."

Shame on me, but I missed it already.

I heard myself say, "Oh, honey, won't you reconsider staying on? They really do need you."

"I'm not sure that God isn't calling me elsewhere, and if so I need to pay attention."

I'm so glad Carl tunes in to the Lord and not me, or he'd be tempted to stay on the board for appearance's sake, for the power and prestige.

For all the wrong reasons.

There went that plumb line again, drifting off with me unaware. The past Sunday during worship I sang "Reign in me" and whispered a prayer from Psalm 139, "Search me, God, and know my heart" (v. 23).

When you ask for a *search me*, you get it.

What a revelation. Let's just slide under the covers, fall back to sleep, and start the morning over again.

Travel back with me to envision Jesus on the mountain pulpit as he describes the qualities of kingdom people. It's the *blessed are those who* . . . beatitudes. Since our Sunday school class is studying the book of Matthew, the question came up recently, "Is he describing who his followers are or what they must do?"

One in the same, we concurred. Thousands gathered on that mountain in Galilee to hear Jesus explain the long-awaited kingdom, yet what they heard about had to do with a lifestyle.

"Blessed are the pure in heart, because they will see God" (Matt. 5:8). The synonyms that pop up in my thesaurus for "pure in heart" are *unworldly* and *holy minded*. Making impressions might gain points in the world but never with God. Then why are we still tempted to do it? We could knead this one all day. The point is, we all enjoy the strokes we get from serving, but danger lurks among all those pats on the back.

We can end up doing what is right in God's eyes for all the wrong reasons.

Like the Pharisees, one of the two major religious groups in Israel at the time of Christ. Admired for their piety, they believed salvation came from perfect obedience to the law, not forgiveness of sin. Oops. No wonder they pondered over every detail in the letter of the law and became more concerned with doing good for appearance's sake.

And their favorite trick? Taking Scripture out of context to point the finger and judge others.

"Be careful not to practice your righteousness in front of people, to be seen by them," Jesus said. "Otherwise, you will have no reward from your Father in heaven" (Matt. 6:2).

Then he warns against being a hypocrite.

These guys thought they could make a big hit with God by complying with outward rules. Jesus told his crowds to *do whatever they tell you but don't copy these characters because they don't do what they say.* "They do everything to be observed by others. They enlarge their phylacteries and lengthen their tassels."

Say what? The word *phylacteries* prompted a search in my Bible dictionary. They were small, animal-skin cubes on leather straps, filled with Scripture quotes, a custom dating back to Deuteronomy, just after Moses gave the commandment to "love with all your heart, soul and strength." Impress them (God's laws) on your hearts, he told his followers; talk about them at home, on the road, and with your children. "Bind them as a sign on your hand and let them be a symbol on your forehead" (Deut. 6:8).

The little boxes were worn by all males over thirteen during morning worship, but the Pharisees opted to make them standard garb, constantly on display. *See me; aren't I the religious one?*

OK, I'm exposing the Pharisees' dirty laundry a bit, but due to my unmasking experience this morning, it seemed fitting to rag on them for a few paragraphs. The word *Pharisee* means "separate," and these guys stretched it to a mistaken extreme. Being *separate* from the world means coming closer to God; it does not mean being set apart as a pious snob. We know they liked being called "Rabbi" by everyone, and they relished the place of honor at banquets and the front seat in the synagogues.

Am I so much different in the way I savor recognition as an elder's wife? I'm blushing right now admitting it.

And don't we all flaunt a phylactery or two? Maybe a T-shirt with a clever slogan, a catchy bumper sticker, or a tote bag—last week in our church bookstore I eyed one with embroidered flowers and a sweet Scripture and picture pockets. We can buy ball caps and money clips, framed art, jewelry, and coffee mugs, hundreds of products to brand us as belonging to Jesus.

And why not? We are his loyal fans.

God told the Jews "to make tassels for the corners of their garments, and put a blue cord . . . at [each] corner. These will serve as tassels for you to look at, so that you may remember all the LORD's commands and obey them and not become unfaithful by following your own heart and your own eyes" (Num. 15:38–39).

Our Bible covers, bracelets, and bric-a-brac should serve the same function, to call to mind our vows to be faithful.

Faithfulness is not an action to get anything from God but to give him honor because he is who he is. "I am the LORD your God who brought you out of the land of Egypt to be your God" (Num. 15:41).

Doing what is right in the Lord's eyes without a humble heart is foolish and brings no real joy.

Carl and I teach a seminar at our church on discovering your spiritual gifts and God's design for you and ministry. Many of the attendees walk in under the myth that *good Christians never say no,* and they're serving at church, filling the slots out of a sense of duty, because "somebody's got to do it," or fear that "if I don't do it, God is not pleased, not to mention the pastor and elders."

They're wearing a nice public smile while nursing a not-so-nice private grudge.

When they leave our class, they're beginning to smile because after four hours of an interactive group, they can dump the guilt on the way out along with their empty coffee cups. God calls us to a ministry that fits our gifts and the dreams he has planted in our hearts. Serving where we are gifted ignites, not exhausts. And it's not always in a prescribed ministry within the church. As someone once said, we aren't leaving the church behind, we're taking the church with us into the world. Serve the Lord with gladness says Psalm 100. But serve him willingly and obey from the heart, and not just for *appearance's sake. . .* when there's no one looking over your shoulder (see Phil. 2:12).

My new friend James Sang Lee, the karate guy, put it this way: "I have the privilege now to serve and follow him out of love rather than duty or responsibility. At times in the faith we can try and work our way to God, and sometimes we try to get by on our own goodness and our own ability. That's work and religion rather than relationship."

Have you been there? Me too.

I'm fond of the book of Joel, three short chapters that changed my life. The central promise is restoration, God pouring out his Spirit in great blessing after loss. However, there is an *if* attached. "If you return to me" (see 2:13). Since embracing this passage of Scripture, I can't pop in my Dean Martin greatest hits CD and hear the song "Return to Me" (repopularized by the movie of the same name) and think of romance. Listen to the lyrics sometime, and hear it as God's love ballad to those he calls his own.

Hurry back, oh my love.

I used to think it meant straightening up my act and doing the right thing, but it goes beyond that. All of us can say we'll repent—turn away and turn back—but how often does the need arise from a fear of the consequences or concern for our reputation or the reality that God won't bless me if I continue with this. *OK, I give in. This road is too bumpy, and it hurts. I'll do it your way.*

It's a beginning, but it doesn't come close to *rending* the heart. That happens when we recognize the slippery slope we're on for what it really is, a grief to God.

Then there is half-baked obedience. We decide which aspects of God's Word to accept and which parts to ignore.

Like Saul, Israel's first king, a tall handsome man with a keen military mind. Humble at first at his anointment to lead his people, pride soon consumed him. Prior to a major battle with the Philistines, the prophet Samuel told Saul to wait with his troops for seven days until he came back to perform a ritual offering to the Lord.

The soldiers had a major meltdown—Scripture says they were "quaking" in fear—and fled for the hills. Saul, anxious to get on with the battle, grew impatient, and when Samuel failed to show up at the appointed time, Saul decided to perform the burnt offering himself. Just then Samuel appeared, railing him for his disobedience.

So began a lifelong conflict with Saul, the man of God, and Saul, the powerful king. After a few more bouts with self-will against God's will, he no longer ruled with God's blessing. That's when Samuel sought out young David who would eventually succeed to the throne.

Saul's constant defense was that he honored God through the proper sacrifices. Samuel smashed that one. "To obey is better than sacrifice, and to heed is better than the fat of rams" (1 Sam. 15:22 NIV). Saul spent more time trying to save face and protect his image than being right with God. He never became God's man and met a tragic end.

King David died at peace with God. His sin—adultery and arranging a murder—had torn him to pieces, not for the tragic consequences it brought, but because it had wounded the God he loved. That's true rending of the heart. Psalm 51 is his moving plea for mercy and forgiveness:

> Wash away my guilt, and cleanse me from
> my sin. For I am conscious of my rebellion, and
> my sin is always before me. Against You—You
> alone—I have sinned and done this evil in Your
> sight. . . .
>
> Surely You desire integrity in the inner self,
> and You teach me wisdom deep within. Purify
> me with hyssop, and I will be clean; wash me,
> and I will be whiter than snow. Let me hear joy
> and gladness; let the bones You have crushed
> rejoice. Turn Your face away from my sins and
> blot out all my guilt. God, create a clean heart
> for me and renew a steadfast spirit within me.
> Do not banish me from Your presence or take
> Your Holy Spirit from me. Restore the joy of
> Your salvation to me, and give me a willing
> spirit. Then I will teach the rebellious Your
> ways, and sinners will return to You.
> (vv. 2–4, 6–13)

Before his death David instructed his son and heir Solomon to make God the center of his life. "I am about to go the way of all the earth," David said in 1 Kings 2:2–3. "So be strong, show yourself a man, and observe what the LORD your God requires: Walk in his ways, and keep his decrees and commands, his laws and requirements . . . so that you may *prosper* in all you do and wherever you go" (NIV).

Prosper, flourish and thrive.

As a friend recently wrote me in an e-mail: "I've been reading David's psalm in *The Message* and praying, "God make a fresh start in me, shape a Genesis week from the chaos of my life." That's one worth borrowing.

David the former shepherd reigned in Jerusalem for thirty-three years and left an honorable and rich heritage for us because, despite his sin and mistakes, he sought to do what was right in God's eyes for the right reasons. And he harkened to the call: *Return to me.*

Do you need to return to the Lord today? He's waiting.

Saying yes to God brings new purpose.

here i am, Lord

chapter 18

When God said, "Arise and go," Jonah hopped a ship to avoid the task of preaching to the wicked folks of Ninevah. So like God to stage a few special effects to bring him to the end of himself.

A storm at sea and a three-day retreat inside a big fish, the type of disasters God rushes to capitalize on, to offer us new revelation. "You threw me into the depths, into the heart of the seas," Jonah prayed in chapter 2, "and the current overcame me. All Your breakers and Your billows swept over me. . . . I sank to the foundations of the mountains; the earth with its prison bars closed behind me forever! But You raised my life from the Pit, LORD my God! . . . As my life was fading away, I remembered the LORD. My prayer came to You, to Your holy temple. . . . I will sacrifice to You with a voice of thanksgiving. *I will fulfill what I have vowed*"(vv. 3, 6–7, 9).

The second time around he chose obedience. As ordered, he preached the message of doom, and everyone in Ninevah turned to God.

Cause for applause and celebration, right? Not for Jonah; he didn't relish seeing those Ninevites forgiven. They were Gentiles, not Jews, Israel's enemies and pagans who should be reaping what they sowed in their corruption. Poor Jonah, he thought God was asking him to do the impossible to reach these people. He focused on God's judgment, not his mercy, and forgot God's character, that he longs for all whom he has created to belong to him, no matter what.

Especially the forgotten ones.

When my new e-mail friend Debbie Roeger read Charles Colson's book *Loving God*, she had no idea it would lead to finding her Ninevah. "I picked up the book not realizing who Chuck Colson was, but with each chapter I felt a tug on my heart. And I thanked God after every chapter that there were those he sent into prisons to minister, but I pleaded with him not to send me there."

As she turned the pages, a seed began to germinate, starting with a memory of a college field trip many years before. Her criminology class visited a medium security prison, Marion Correctional Institution in Ohio. "To this day I have a clear sense of the intense emotion that welled up inside me at the helpless despair on the faces of the inmates," she told me. "I left the place depressed and frightened, and while God planted a seed of compassion in my heart for those behind bars, I chose to run the other way. After all, I reasoned, the problem is just too big. I'd rather play it safe."

By the time she closed the book, Debbie knew God was stirring her heart again. "This time I decided to respond. The book introduced me to the concept of retirement home residents writing to prison inmates, so I contacted Prison Fellowship Ministries and gathered information on Mail Call. Once I delivered the information to the program director at the home, I felt good; I had met my obligation."

But God had other plans for this goal-driven attorney and practicing mediator.

At lunch one day Debbie's friend asked her, "What do you do to maintain an intimate relationship with God?"

"She caught me off guard. I had to admit that I really didn't have *that* kind of relationship, and I found myself asking her forgiveness for the hypocrisy that made it seem like I did. It so shook me up that I went to my knees in repentance that evening and sought God in a brand-new way. Though saved when I was nine years old, I had never developed intimacy with Christ. Through my tears I told him that I would *go anywhere or do anything* he asked of me. I just wanted to be one with him."

Arise and go. "The message was as specific as Jonah's. God was calling me to go to the Marion Correctional Institution and serve him there. I tried all the excuses I could think of to get God to change his mind. *God, what do I have to offer? They won't accept me, I've never been an inmate. I don't even know any inmates. God, I can still hear the sound of the bars closing and echoing in the hallways from thirty years before. It's such a scary place! I don't even know anyone involved in prison ministry. Did I hear you correctly, God? Did I make this up?*"

Her then-seventeen-year-old daughter set her straight on that one. "Mom," she said with a firm gaze, "does that sound like the kind of thing you would make up?"

"I had to admit," Debbie added, "that if I was going to create a vision of what God had in mind for me, it would not be in a prison, and a men's prison at that. *God, did you notice that you made me a woman?*"

She thought of Ananias when the Lord told him of Saul's conversion on Damascus Road and called him to be the one to open the future apostle's blind eyes. "He uttered something like, *God, do you know his reputation? Do you know why he came here, Lord? Do you know what he has done? How can someone like that become a Christian? Not me, Lord, can't you send someone else?*"

Debbie had a choice to make. "Obedience or disobedience, and there was no gray area. Would I bury once again the compassion that God had uncovered in my heart from so long ago, knowing that if I did, I would miss God's best for me?"

She walked and talked and prayed and cried. "Until finally in my heart the answer would be *yes, Lord!* At that moment God began to prepare me for all he would call me to do in prison."

First, she was called to pray for all the men she would meet, and part of her prayer was that "I be acceptable to them."

Then she was called to resign her job, "which I dearly loved, maybe more than I loved the Lord at the time. I don't mind telling you it was a tough decision. I ached at the loss of my professional identity; it had defined who I was all of my adult life. God knew that it was a sacrifice I needed to make to be fully restored to him."

Three months later she found herself at the second annual Justice Fellowship Conference on restorative justice in Washington, D.C. "I had registered just two days before, telling my husband, *I don't know why I need to be there. I just know God is sending me.*"

She used the time at the conference to concentrate on hearing the voice of God concerning her future. "I'd return to my hotel room, get on my knees, and pray that God would reveal to me why he had called me here. By the afternoon of the second day, my prayers were answered."

She heard about a pilot program, an interfaith dorm that would house forty-eight men of different faiths—Christian, Jewish, and Muslim—giving them an opportunity to grow in respect and tolerance for other faiths.

How fascinating, she thought. "What prison will be piloting that program?"

Marion Correctional Institution in Ohio. "As soon as I heard that, I knew why I was at the conference." By the time she returned home, she had an introduction to the prison warden. "I remember sitting in her office as she described with great passion a need for volunteers to assist with a program that allowed the children of inmates to visit their fathers for a day, a day with a variety of fun activities planned. Could I help? I swallowed hard, not wanting to appear ungrateful for the opportunity, but politely replied that, well, working with children was not really my gift. The warden looked confused and exasperated."

Meanwhile, Debbie prayed silently, *Show me what to do, God. I know you have called me here. Show me what it is you want me to do.*

And God prompted her: *Tell her your background and experience.* "I have my master's in human resources management, and I've practiced law for eleven years. I'm trained as a mediator, although I've taken early retirement to begin a private mediation practice."

The warden's eyes grew wide as she broke out in a smile. "Would you be willing to volunteer here using your mediation skills?"

"Absolutely."

"Would it matter if you work with staff or inmates?"

Whatever you want, Lord.

The warden slid her hand under her desk blotter. "For the past two years I've kept this brochure about mediation, fully intending to do something about it someday. I suspect that the *someday* is here."

Within days Debbie was commissioned to help with the very interfaith pilot program that had been explained at the life-changing conference in Washington. By any chance, would she be willing to design the dispute resolution model that would be used by the dorm?

Willing was an understatement. Her work at the prison had begun with exuberance.

"It's almost mind-boggling to look back over the past nineteen months to see what we've accomplished here," Debbie said. Training inmates to mediate their own disputes, starting a faith-based conflict management class, setting up accountability partners, designing programs that build teamwork, and much more.

"I know God is preparing me to follow him to other prisons," she added. By the time you read this, Debbie will have worked with Christian inmates in an Arizona prison pilot program. And she does it all as a volunteer under a nonprofit ministry called Opening Doors of Ohio, Inc. "It is God's call on my life in this season."

And the fruits of her efforts are not solely for others. There is lasting spiritual nourishment that comes with what Jesus calls "doing the will of him who sent me."

"God has used my area of service to call me more closely to himself," she said, "to heal me of deep wounds. I tried all the self-help books but never experienced true victory in my life until Jesus became the passion and love of my life. He showed me clearly the trap Satan had set for me as a driven woman desiring success in the professional world. I fell for it at great cost. But thanks be to God that he is still in the redemption business. And it is never too late in our lives to turn to him and begin to walk in radical obedience."

The ultimate expression of our love for God.

When I posted a message about my new book subject to my writers' online group, Tricia responded. "I have a great obedience story," she wrote. "Five years ago my pastor (and friend) asked me to help start a pregnancy center in my area. My first response was *no way*. I was a writer, and I had plans, goals, and dreams, but I told him at least I would pray about it."

At the time she had just started an *Experiencing God* study at church. "A few key phrases stuck with me. 'See what God is doing and join him there.' Also, *'God has the plan, he'll do the work. He just needs willing servants to follow'* (author's paraphrase). Then I started thinking about it. My writing was going nowhere. Every door had shut. In fact, I had a go-ahead for a children's book series, and they had backed out of it."

But she was busy leading a Bible study for women who had been through the abortion experience, and lives were being transformed. "Then I was approached about the center. Could this be God at work, I wondered?"

A thought kept popping into her head: *What are you doing to reach the people in your community?* And my friend Joanna says, "When a thought pops into our head and it's too wise to be us, then it's usually God."

Starting a center was not even close to what she wanted to do. "It was like a knife to my heart, cutting through my pride. But when I looked around at what God was doing in my midst, I came to the conclusion that it must be his plan and he would make it happen."

And he did. Tricia put her writing dreams in storage and plunged into starting the center. "After six months we were fully functional, and two years later we were offering all the services of a professional center. In 2003 we reached more than two thousand clients, and the abortion rate decreased by one-third in our community.

"And it didn't stop there but mushroomed into a school abstinence education program, tangible resources for teen moms, and stirred passions inside of me I didn't know existed. As a woman who had an abortion at age fifteen and a child at seventeen, I've also found amazing healing as I've helped others heal. I'm so glad God knows and loves us so much that he'll push us into his good plans."

Today there are two paid staff positions at the center and fifty volunteers. Tricia serves on the board of directors and works with the teen moms. "That's it," she says. "I'm busy writing." Once the center was up and running, God gave Tricia the desire of her heart, a contract for a novel. "And the contracts have continued steadily ever since. I feel that since I was obedient, trusting God and taking him at his word, he took care of me."

As Andrew Murray said in *The Blessings of Obedience,* "Give him all and he will give you all."[1]

It's the end result of the undivided heart—whole, complete, and lacking in nothing, a heart willing and ready to go when God calls, a heart ripe for the goodness that will come.

Through endurance we conquer.

volunteers needed

chapter 19

It was the golden age of exploration, and Sir Ernest Shackleton had a dream to be the first to cross the Antarctic continent and bring the glory to England. Needing volunteers for the expedition, he placed this brutally honest ad in the newspaper:

> Men wanted for hazardous journey. Small wages,
>> bitter cold, long months of complete darkness,
>> constant danger.
> Safe return doubtful. Honor and recognition in
>> case of success.

For the twenty-seven spots available, he was flooded with five thousand applications.

Before departing with his handpicked scientists and seamen, Shackleton visited with the king of England, who lamented, "It is terrible to be responsible for the lives of so many."

A foretelling statement if ever there was one. In December 1914, just one day's sail from the continent, the wooden ship became trapped in the icy jaws of the Weddell Sea. For ten months she drifted in a frozen vise grip that finally crushed her to pieces.

The men now faced the stark reality of "constant danger and return doubtful." Castaways in a strange and hostile place, they had no radio contact, and no help was on the way. It was up to their boss to lead his men to safety, and the records show that it was at this very moment Irish-born Sir Ernest Shackleton showed his greatness. Unrelenting courage and determined optimism that he would bring every man back alive. Their well-being—mental, physical, emotional—took priority over everything else.

Early last year I taped the A&E movie called *Shackelton*, one of the most incredible adventure stories ever told, and when we finally watched it that summer, it was yet another window through which God spoke.

Shackleton had renamed his ship *Endurance* after his family motto: *Fortitudine Vincimus—Through endurance we conquer*. And while the vessel didn't stand up to the strain, he did. To help his crew deal with the trauma of being stranded, Shackleton became the servant, rising early in the morning to make hot milk and hand-delivering it to every tent in the temporary camp. He diligently checked every man for possible frostbite. And on a freezing open-boat journey to search for a way out, he gave a suffering comrade his gloves.

Emulating their boss, the crew cared for one another and boosted morale. Gone was the tendency to lie, cheat, and look out for number one to survive. It was as if the *Endurance* wasn't lost in another polar region but found in a new universe.

One where self-sacrifice replaces self-interest.

Shackleton never minimized the danger; he spoke the truth about their plight, but he proved to be such an outstanding leader that his men refused to let their circumstances defeat them. Sir Ernest never had to enforce obedience. The men followed him wholeheartedly, or else they would have perished. Not only was he their commander but also a teacher and visionary who challenged them to rise to their best.

And it made all the difference.

OK, where are you going with this, Jan? you might wonder. Aside from encouraging you to see the film, there is a point. Once Shackleton understood his mission—and died to his dream of personal triumph and national glory—he turned his energy toward the necessary goal. I see God's hand in his life as every past experience forged in him the character and strength he would need for the seemingly impossible task ahead.

God's hand is on us in the very same way.

We are his go-betweens, the conduits through which he wants to lead and encourage others to believe in what human eyes cannot see. In a strange and wonderful way, we're his modern-day prophets. They seldom won popularity contests, these impassioned oracles. What a job, speaking truth and calling people to righteousness but with the promise of forgiveness and renewal.

First there was Moses, shaped by God to lead the exodus from Egypt, who brings the Israelites the Ten Commandments. *God does his greatest deeds through flawed and insecure people.*

Elijah, in his unique, fervent style, proclaimed the one true God. *Remain loyal, and you'll have a great impact on your world.*

Elisha, the healer and prophet of miracles. *God cares about your every need.*

Joel, "Jehovah is God," urges the self-centered heart to make a U-turn. *Return to the Lord, and he will restore the dreams the locusts have devoured.*

Hosea, whose name means "salvation," grieves over an unfaithful wife. *God will love you and woo you back to himself no matter what.*

Isaiah, prophet to a nation divided, has a vision of the future. *The Savior is coming to set up his kingdom.* "He was pierced for our transgressions, . . . crushed for our iniquities" (Isa. 53:5 NIV).

Jeremiah, prophet of disaster and doom, was strengthened by years of personal obedience. "I set you apart before you were born. Do not be afraid for I will be with you."

Ezekiel, priest to the exiles, displays the unchangeable strength and holiness of God. "I will cleanse you from all your impurities. . . . I will give you a new heart and put a new spirit in you; I will remove your heart of stone and give you a heart of flesh" (Ezek. 36:25–26).

And last on my list: John the Baptist, the fearless street preacher who paves the way for Jesus' coming. "The crooked will become straight, the rough ways smooth, and everyone will see the salvation of God" (Isa. 40:4–5).

The angel announcing his birth to Zechariah said that John was being set apart for God's service, and he had but one mission in life: "To shine on those who live in darkness and the shadow of death, to guide our feet into the way of peace" (Luke 1:79).

And he threw himself into it with zeal.

When John baptized Jesus in the Jordan River, the heavens opened up, and the Lord's ministry on earth officially began. Jesus later said, "Among those born of women no one greater than John the Baptist has appeared" (Matt. 11:11). And no one more humble—"He is the One coming after me, whose sandal strap I'm not worthy to untie" (John 1:27)—or more uncompromising.

I ask myself this question: Are you willing to be a John the Baptist in somebody's life, pointing others to the Savior? Not that we need to wrap ourselves in camel hair and stop off at the organic market for locusts and honey or go around confronting, "You brood of vipers." (Though I witnessed a few eccentric crack-pots preaching just that on the K Street Mall near the capitol building on my lunch hour. And no potential converts came very close.)

Are you willing to be a voice crying in the wilderness? We live in an era when the world is seeking answers to the age-old question about meaning and purpose, and there's a host of false prophets who speak from their own misguided truth and not the

Lord's, who lead many far off the mark and straight into the dark.

Some of us are lost ourselves, and we need other prophets to come alongside and help us find our way back to the kingdom.

Will we step out for God and say *use me?* Or when it starts to hurt—as it always will—say, "I'm just not up to it, Lord; find somebody else," and retreat to our comfort zone.

I know that place. It's cozy and convenient and well guarded, a gated community on Easy Street, and I still have the password hidden. I've entered there many times hoping, like Jonah, to lay low while God reassigns the hard tasks to somebody else.

You're reading a book I hoped not to write. Blame it on Carl. After one of those challenging sessions with counselor Ken, he said, "This should be your next book about *kingdom living* and obedience and doing the right thing."

OK, sounds intriguing. All morning we played idea football, tossing and punting thoughts around. "What if you explored this truth," he said: "If we truly love God, we'll trust him, trust that he has our best in mind *always*. It's then that we can stand firm and follow his commands."

"And do the right thing—whether we're confused, feel abandoned, or stand to lose everything."

"That's it, doing the right thing with confidence, no matter what."

"Even if we're shaking in our boots." Like I often do.

"It's a perfect follow-up book to *After the Locusts*," he added.

I gave a firm nod and scribbled some notes. "As we partner with God toward restoration, we face more temptation to take the easy way out of our pain and disappointment." Been there, done that with gusto.

"It's our job to find out what's right, do it, and leave the results to God." Well said, Carl.

What a concept, so I went to work on a killer book proposal, penning lofty words like these: *Standing for Christ brings great reward: an unshakeable faith that won't wobble when the storms come, a faith that won't bend with fickle feelings, a faith that brings peace and fulfillment, something we all want, something that only comes with having the mind of Christ.*

It elevates our relationship with him to a new height, one that sees through his eyes and never looks back.

That was two years ago, and when a contract didn't materialize right away, I thought, *Oh good, maybe I don't have to do it after all.* It dawned on me: *Write a book about obedience? What was I thinking? Who wants to explore that one? Let Carl write the thing; it was his brainchild in the first place.* I had several more projects in circulation, so this one washed right out of my mind.

And last year at a writers' conference, my agent and I lingered in the coffee lounge. "Who knows why all your writing projects are stalled," she said, melting my mood. "God must be up to something."

I pursed my lips. *That's for sure.* The past eight months had been filled with epiphanies, burning bush moments of revelation, struggles that brought to light how God calls me to have the right attitude and do the right thing no matter whether I feel slighted, cheated, or overlooked.

No wonder God delayed the approval for this book; he had some lessons to teach me before I tackled this important topic.

Not to focus on "obedience" as corrective discipline or what my counselor friend Ken calls "the gospel of sin management," that breeds only a bunch of guilt. It's not about focusing on the "doing" but on what our lives are supposed to be about, developing a mind-set that captures your heart and spreads to your hands and feet to get you moving in a holy direction. Then doing the right thing comes naturally out of our organic passions.

It's about coming to the place where the things that break God's heart also break ours.

And about taking the time to be still and know that he is God, and getting in touch with a generous and loving Savior.

It's about kingdom living with the Christian worldview.

Many of the stories in previous chapters deal with letting go of self-will and surrendering to God's will. Do we learn to love God first and then we can move aside the obstacles to surrender, or does the very act of surrender even under protest produce a surprising and incredible love for the one we surrender to?

We've seen both. When God finally reveals himself, there is only one response; we fall on our knees and say, "Here I am, Lord. I want to hear what you are saying. Tell me what you desire of me."

When it comes to those black-and-white issues like sex outside of marriage, being yoked with unbelievers, lying, stealing, swearing, or pushing your Christian daughter toward divorce, God's will is as clear as Saran Wrap.

But what about those gray areas that Scripture doesn't address? If only angels would come to us in a dream, like Joseph when he discovered Mary was pregnant. After deciding to divorce her secretly out of respect, the angel gave him a heads-up about the future of the baby to come.

There are no crystal balls, but this I know: the closer you draw to God, the more you learn to distinguish his voice.

In the movie *The Passion of the Christ*, Jesus told Pilate, "All men who hear the truth hear my voice."

Years ago I heard a sermon on discovering God's will, and it saved me when I fell into infatuation with an old flame from high school. Strolling down memory lane, we reached out to each other to recapture our innocence, and for a while it felt like God's perfect plan.

Do I marry him or not? He's crazy about me, and though he hasn't been a Christian long, he seems to love you, Lord.

I quizzed myself just as the sermon directed: Have you checked God's Word? *Yes, it's not really applicable here as we're both Christians.*

Would you feel right asking God to bless it? *Yes indeed.* Could you thank him for it? *I've been single-again for eight years!* Would it be a stumbling block to others? *Don't think so.* Do the circumstances line up? *I met him again through my daughter. How's that for an unex-pected open door?* Have you sought godly counsel or advice, those who have a track record of experience, with no personal stake in your decision? *Oops, not really. Only my friend Jeanne, who hasn't pointed out any red flags yet, but she thinks he's a hunk. We're attending a premarriage group right now at his church, but nobody knows me there. Maybe I should consult with Bruce. He'll give me the straight scoop.*

Would the decision be to God's glory? *Now that's a hard one. I would hope so.* Will your decision or actions bring you closer to God or pull you farther away? *Now we're getting into the sticky stuff. We disagree on some practical issues like money and debt. And I'm trying to grow him up in the faith real fast, buying books and tapes for him. In thinking it over, I'm more concerned with his spiritual growth than my own right now. And he's pressing for marriage soon because "it's better to marry than to burn with passion." I've had to become the moral compass in our relationship, which isn't too much fun.*

Have you sought the Lord about it? *M'mm, not in the way I should.*

And last: Do you have a sense of peace? *Not really, there's a check in my spirit, and I'm trying to pretend it is just the jitters, trying to convince myself he just needs to feel secure and he'll stop hanging on so tight and pressuring me.*

My spirit's nudging told me that we had gone ahead of God and were not ready to be engaged. After explaining the reasons, he peered at me. "You are not listening and following God's will. He told me we are to be together."

But he hasn't told me.

More pressure led to a bitter breakup. He has not spoken with me since. Weeks later, after the pain of missing him lessened,

I trusted that God was saving me for something far better, for my good and his ultimate glory.

Asking the right questions and heeding my heart's reply served me well. When Carl came along, our relationship passed the test.

The chief end of man, according to the Westminster Catechism, is to glorify God and enjoy him forever. To *glorify* is to praise and honor him with our obedience, and then *enjoy*—receive pleasure from our Creator, bask in his wonder, and revel in his goodness.

Do the right thing as he has revealed it to you, and the rewards will be to enjoy him forever.

One of our biggest barriers to obedience is impatience. It runs neck and neck with the divided heart. And since the beginning when we were driven out of paradise, we get antsy in God's waiting room. In our quick-fix drive-through, microwave society, waiting is almost a lost art. When God doesn't move fast enough to suit our needs or delays his directives after we labor in prayer, we get weary and seize control. *I can't just sit here. I have to make something happen to change this situation.*

"To lose patience," said Gandhi, "is to lose the battle."

If obedience is God's answer to our problem, patience rates high as a remedy for the yet unsolved dilemmas in life. If we choose courage—"I am able to do all things through Him who strengthens me" (Phil. 4:13)—and wait it out, God will make the most of the time and form us for great purpose. Standing up for Christ ensures one thing, that we'll have our lion's share of troubles, but I like to remember what they produce in our lives—endurance.

"The testing of your faith produces endurance. But endurance must do its complete work, so that you may be mature and complete, lacking nothing" (James 1:3–4).

I wonder if Sir Ernest Shackleton knew that verse.

"To endure is greater than to dare," said William Thackeray, "to be daunted by no difficulty, to keep heart when all have lost it, to go through intrigue spotless, to forego even ambition when the end is gained—who can say this is not greatness."

Through endurance we conquer.

And now for the rest of the Shackleton story. When their ice camp broke up, the men piled into boats and eventually reached the tiny, rocky, and barren Elephant Island, far from civilization. Sir Ernest set off with five others across one of the roughest seas in the world to get help at the South Georgia Island whaling station—eight hundred miles away. They finally landed, but on the wrong side of the island, and had to cross mountains, glaciers, and snowfields on foot with no proper gear.

Only guts.

They organized a rescue team and finally returned for the remaining crew, men who had lived on seal meat, birds, and hope for twenty-two harsh months.

And every man was alive.

The history books call Sir Ernest Shackleton many things— ruthless and ambitious, an unabashed adventurer, an inspired leader, a glorious failure. None of it matters to me. His is an example of extraordinary endurance, the kind we need as Christians, to weather the storms, beat the odds, scale the mountains, and cross the Rubicons in our lives.

To stand firm and devoted until the end despite anything life hurls at us.

"Endurance," said William Barclay, "is not just the ability to bear a hard thing, but to turn it into glory."

conclusion

If only we had Shackelton's fearless determination. Most of us connect more with Moses, who cowered during God's call at the burning bush: *Lord, who am I to do this thing?* Or Peter, who abandoned his good intentions: *They caught me off guard, and fear took over.* Or David, lusting after a beautiful woman on a rooftop: *I know I should be out with my men in battle, but this is too tempting.* Or Rahab, living outside the edge of acceptability *because of my circumstances.*

But once each embraced a God worth loving enough to trust completely, they found the courage to risk for him and became new folks with new focus.

Remembering this perks me up like a Frappachino.

About a month ago our Sunday school class tackled this pithy issue—the heart as a life force and the path from the carnal to the pure. As dozens of thumbs leafed through Bibles searching for Scriptures to share, I fired up my fountain pen ready to take notes on a rich grab bag of comments and contradictions.

Our class is a no-holds-barred, anything-goes place, and the conversation was lively. The wicked heart, the renewed heart, and what exactly does circumcising the heart really mean? How much is up to us? Do we give Satan too much credit? Isn't pride our real enemy? Why aren't Christians profoundly different from the world? What is the *kingdom* within us?

Hey guys, you don't know it, but you're writing the end of my book.

We all agreed that Psalm 24:3–5 summed it up: "Who may ascend the mountain of the LORD? Who may stand in His holy place? The one who has clean hands and a pure heart, who has not set his mind on what is false, and who has not sworn deceitfully."

Diane shares often, and everyone appreciates her unreserved, off-the-record disclosures. "I know I'm saved, but the more I step out in faith, the harder it is. Am I the only one to struggle with wrong desires?"

No, we all are tempted. The battle is real. Satan's troops will do their best to deceive us. Bombard us with disbelief.

"Then how do we achieve the weapons to fight?" someone asked.

We have to stand on what the Word says, that we are holy. Direct our minds to the right things. God will empower us to walk according to the Spirit.

Teacher Hal said, "Jesus didn't ascend into heaven and say, 'Now you're on your own.'" And Bruce, our Vietnam veteran, added, "In war, there's a buddy to your rear and at your side and ahead of you. It is the comradeship that bonds you and makes you fight harder."

According to our resident military buff, having battle-field buddies tranquilizes the nervous system. "It makes all the difference in the world whether you can do your job or not. As believers, we must stay in fellowship."

Bingo.

It is when we feel alone or abandoned that hearts grow weary and faint and the battle becomes too hard.

I looked around the room, a jigsaw puzzle of people—all ages, all styles. John in his motorized wheelchair, constantly smiling, raising his hand to share as he labors to speak due to cerebral palsy. Young and old, single and married, with differing opinions and perspectives but with one common thread—a desire for truth and the passion to live for the glory of God.

That's inspiring. Each week we journey together, bearing one anothers' burdens, challenging one another to God's best no matter what.

Do you have such a group or a few friends with single-minded devotion who constantly move toward the ancient path, where the *good way is,* and will encourage you to walk in it? Expect to be misunderstood and criticized when you stand for the Lord, when you choose a way that seems foolish to the human eye. Unshakeable friends will be your buffer.

Abraham Lincoln said, "Stand with anybody that stands right. Stand with him while he is right, and part with him when he goes wrong." There's wisdom in that, and wisdom, God says, is "sweet to your soul" (Prov. 24:14 NIV).

"Direct me in the path of your commands, for there I find delight" (Ps. 119:35 NIV).

You may need to ask God to remove any barriers to obedience, any remnants—old skeletons of failures, grudges, grief—left over from the past. In Philippians 3:14, Paul tells us to forget what is behind and reach forward to what is ahead. The goal is the promised prize of our heavenly call in Christ.

If this book says anything, it's that we cannot follow God with a partial heart. He wants it all, and he infuses the power we need to hand it over. And sometimes, as with me, he must break a stubborn heart so we might choose his right path.

But the rewards are worth the strain and pain.

"I will plant them and not uproot them. I will give them a heart to know Me, that I am the LORD. They will be my people, and I will be their God because they will return to Me with all their heart" (Jer. 24:6–7).

Don't ever give up if you think you've failed God. It's like encountering the roundabout, those curious traffic circles in

England with exit roads jetting out like spikes. The first time we found ourselves in one, we had just escaped from the madness of London traffic. I was relishing the sheep in green pastures when Carl, trying to stay focused on his wrong-side-of-the-road driving, squeaked, "Jan, we're coming to a roundabout. What do I do?"

As designated navigator, I fumbled for the maps that didn't give me an immediate clue. "I don't know."

"Well, hurry up, I'm about to enter this thing."

Cars beeped at these frustrated tourists as we tried to merge. "Jan, what do I do?"

"Just get into that inner circle until I figure this out." Good thing I noticed the little skirt of safety inside the *sphere of frustration*. So there we were going round and round like fools, me trying to figure out which color-coded road to take. There are main roads, secondary roads, historical landmark roads, and they only indicate the next town, not our ultimate destination, Yorkshire.

"Oh, just take a left."

"Jan, they are all left turns!" I'd never seen Carl so frazzled before. By the time we ventured out of the roundabout, we both decided that if we ever come to Great Britain again we're taking the train.

We opted for the wrong exit and after a few miles had to turn around to face the dreaded roundabout again. But this time it had a more comforting look. We knew that the inner circle would always be there in a confused moment. We could tuck in there, take a breath, and get our bearings before heading out again.

There is always a way back to God. His unending love is the inner circle of safety. He doesn't care where we've been or what we've done, only where we are heading now.

If God were to run a newspaper ad, this is what it would say:

WANTED

Men and women for hazardous journey.

Long years of trials and tribulation. Constant testing.

Honor and glory in this life not guaranteed.

Eternal blessings for those who trust and obey.

notes

Chapter Two

1. Henry T. Blackaby and Claude King, *Experiencing God: Knowing and Doing the Will of God* (Nashville, Tenn.: LifeWay Press, 1990), 109.

2. Ibid., 126.

3. Ibid., 128.

Chapter Three

1. Dennis Rainey interview at www.beliefnet.com/story/51/story.

Chapter Four

1. Cecil Murphey, *The Relentless God* (Grand Rapids, Mich.: Bethany House, 2003), 13.

Chapter Five

1. Adapted from the *Renovaré Perspective Newsletter*, available at www.renovare.org.

2. Compiled by Edythe Draper, *Draper's Quotations for the Christian World* (Wheaton, Ill.: Tyndale, 1993), 8109.

Chapter Nine

1. Dallas Willard, *Renovation of the Heart* (Colorado Springs, Colo.: Navpress, 2002), 65.

2. Greg Asimakoupoulos, "Sacrificing Success," *Stand Firm*, March 2002, 6–7.

Chapter Ten

1. www.brandonslay.com.

2. www.fca.org.

3. Eric Tiansay, "Internal Power," www.fca.org, 14 January 2004.

Chapter Thirteen

1. Ken Gire, *Windows of the Soul* (Grand Rapids, Mich.: Zondervan, 1996), 118.

2. Ibid., 120

3. Dallas Willard, *Renovation of the Heart* (Colorado Springs, Colo.: NavPress, 2002), 95.

4. Matt Schnepf, "Donna Rice Hughes—Enough Is Enough," *Light and Life*, January/February 2004, 16.

Chapter Fourteen

1. Bob Jones, "The Reluctant Hero," *World Magazine*, February 2002.

2. Charles Colson, *Born Again* (Grand Rapids, Mich.: Baker, 1983), 155.

3. Quoted from "Conversion of Watergate Figure Charles Colson," www.gospelcom.net, 12 August 2002.

4. Article by Chuck Colson on the Postmodern Crack-up as excerpted on www.christianitytoday.com, 2 December 2003.

5. As quoted on www.mcjonline.com/news.

Chapter Eighteen

1. Andrew Murray, *The Blessings of Obedience* (New Kensington, Pa.: Whitaker House, 2002), 83.

about the author

Jan Coleman is an author and popular speaker at conferences, women's retreats, banquets, and teas. She challenges and motivates her audiences to take the high road with God. Visit her Web site at www.jancoleman.com. She would love to hear from you.